# PRAYER
## *Conversations with God*

---

### Dr. Samuel Bulgin

*To The Cordner's Family with Best Wishes*

*Samuel Bulgin*

*1-22-18*

**TEACH Services, Inc.**
P U B L I S H I N G
www.TEACHServices.com • (800) 367-1844

World rights reserved. This book or any portion thereof may not be copied or reproduced in any form or manner whatever, except as provided by law, without the written permission of the publisher, except by a reviewer who may quote brief passages in a review.

The author assumes full responsibility for the accuracy of all facts and quotations as cited in this book. The opinions expressed in this book are the author's personal views and interpretations, and do not necessarily reflect those of the publisher.

This book is provided with the understanding that the publisher is not engaged in giving spiritual, legal, medical, or other professional advice. If authoritative advice is needed, the reader should seek the counsel of a competent professional.

Except where otherwise noted, all Scripture quotations are from the Holy Bible, New King James Version Copyright 1979, 1980, 1982, HarperCollins. Used by permission of Thomas Nelson Publishers.

*The Holy Bible New International Version®*. (NIV). Copyright © 1973, 1978, 1984 by International Bible Society. All rights reserved.

*The Holy Bible, New Century Version®*. (NCV) Copyright © 2005 by Thomas Nelson, Inc. Holman Christian Standard Bible (HCSB)

Copyright © 1999, Berean Study Bible (BSB) © 2016, 2018 by Bible Hub and Berean. Bible. Used by Permission. All rights Reserved. Free downloads and licensing available. See also the Berean Literal Bible and Berean Interlinear Bible. 2000, 2002, 2003, 2009 by Holman Bible Publishers, Nashville Tennessee. All rights reserved.

---

Copyright © 2019 Dr. Samuel Bulgin
Copyright © 2019 TEACH Services, Inc.
ISBN-13: 978-1-4796-1005-1 (Paperback)
ISBN-13: 978-1-4796-1006-8 (ePub)
Library of Congress Control Number: 2018962301

Scripture quotations marked The Message are taken from The Message. Copyright © 1993, 1994, 1995, 1996, 2000, 2001, 2002. Used by permission of NavPress Publishing Group.

Scripture quotations marked NASB are taken from the New American Standard Bible®, copyright © 1960, 1962, 1963, 1968, 1971, 1972, 1973, 1975, 1977, 1995 by The Lockman Foundation. Used by permission.

Scripture quotations marked NIV are taken from The Holy Bible, New International Version®, NIV®. Copyright © 1973, 1978, 1984, 2011 by Biblica, Inc™. Used by permission. All rights reserved world wide.

Texts credited to NKJV are taken from the New King James Version®. Copyright © 1982 by Thomas Nelson, Inc. Used by permission. All rights reserved.

Scripture quotations marked NLT are taken from the Holy Bible, New Living Translation, copyright © 1996, 2004, 2007 by Tyndale House Foundation. Used by permission of Tyndale House Publishers, Inc., Carol Stream, Illinois 60188. All rights reserved.

Scripture quotations marked REB are taken from The Revised English Bible, copyright © Cambridge University Press and Oxford University Press 1989. All rights reserved.

# CONTENTS

Introduction .................................................................................. v
Chapter 1. Prayer ........................................................................ 7
Chapter 2. To Whom Do We Pray? ............................................ 16
Chapter 3. A Perfect Prayer Pattern ............................................ 24
Chapter 4. Prayer and Faith ........................................................ 29
Chapter 5. Unhindered Prayer .................................................... 33
Chapter 6. Prayer and Spirituality .............................................. 43
Chapter 7. Authentic Prayers ...................................................... 50
Chapter 8. Lessons for Fathers from a Model Prayer ................ 56
Chapter 9. Don't Be Anxious! Just Pray .................................... 65
Chapter 10. Prayer in Everything ............................................... 70
Chapter 11. Listen—God is Speaking ........................................ 76
Chapter 12. Prayer and God's Will ............................................. 82
Chapter 13. What If God Answered All Your Prayers? ............. 90

# INTRODUCTION

You might ask, "Why another book on prayer? There are so many on the market already." My answer is simple. At a recent gathering of pastors, we were reminded of the importance of journaling as a part of our devotional life and in the preparation of sermons, so I started journaling. Subsequent to that beginning, I shared one of my entries with a prayer group at the church and the ministry director wanted to know if I could let her know where she could get a copy. I smiled and said, "That's from something I've been writing as I study and reflect on the importance of prayer in my devotional life."

So, though it is not intended to become a national best seller, yet the fact that that dear lady wanted to read it and that you are reading it now is satisfaction enough. If your prayer life can be transformed or simply strengthened by this book, it would be worth the effort.

You might be interested to know that I have carried the document around on my phone and, at different times, as I have read and reflected on it, the person's question has come to mind, "Can I get a copy of it?" Thus have I taken this step to make it available not only to her but to anyone interested in reading more on the subject.

I had another concern: What would I title it? My other books have a variation of the word "divine," so the title, *Prayer: Divine Communication*, seemed a natural first step. Yet, it didn't seem to fit. *Prayer: Communications with God* sounded good to me, though I had never asked anyone else's opinion. I emailed the document to Annette Boyd, my administrative assistant, who had agreed to format it for me. When she completed the first draft, she added the title, *Prayer: Conversations with God*. I could not believe it. It had to be a "God thing." So here you are, holding what was for her a life-changing document. I hope it will do for you as it has done for my administrative assistant and me. If you are blessed by it, share it with a friend. I will be forever grateful.

Many thanks to my wife, Roseclaire, and to our children, Dr. Lee Bulgin and his wife Hadassah and Paul.

# CHAPTER 1

# PRAYER

Prayer is an unnatural activity for men, given to the idea of self-reliance. "Prayer is alien to our proud human nature. And yet somewhere, someplace, probably all of us reach the point of falling on our knees, bowing our heads, fixing our attention on God and praying" (Bill Hybels, *Too Busy Not to Pray*, p. 9). Self-reliance and belief in God cannot co-exist in the human heart. Think about what the writer of Hebrews says: "But without faith it is impossible to please him: for he who comes to God must believe that He is, and that He is a rewarder of those who diligently seek Him" (Heb. 11:6).

> *Prayer is alien to our proud human nature*

God will not compete with our spirit of self-reliance. We will not go to God while self is enthroned in our thinking. Why pray to a God who we do not believe exists or we do not believe is able to do exceedingly abundantly above all that we are able to ask or think (Eph. 3:20, 21)? Belief in God makes the unnatural natural. When we believe in God, we see Him for who He is and are excited to build a stronger relationship with Him. The stronger the relationship, the more intimate it is.

## Prayer is being intimate with God

We all crave intimacy. We all want someone with whom we can connect at the deepest level. God takes our relationship with Him seriously. Relationship is so important to Him that He is willing to be reckless with His grace. While we were still His active enemy, His Son died for us, and He accepted us into His family as children with all of the risk that acceptance involves. This is probably the reason that John, who experienced His love, could not reflect on it without exclaiming, "Behold what manner of love the Father has bestowed on us, that we should be called children of God! Therefore the world does not know us, because it did not know Him" (1 John 3:1).

In our broken world, the more that others know about us, the less they love us. Yet, God who knows everything about us loves us much more than we are sometimes willing to accept. How many times has a spouse said, "I feel like I'm in love with someone I don't know"? They have come upon knowledge about their spouse that they never thought existed, and their love is called into question. They have difficulty communicating. However, in order to experience deep intimacy, communication is always a must.

## Prayer is the avenue through which we experience deep intimacy with God

If this is so, it means that communication is indispensable. Meaningful communication is open, honest, and constructive. God is the only person who knows everything about us, while loving us to the point of giving His life for us. So, we need not hide from Him, even though it is our nature to want to hide. When Adam sinned, his first impulse was to hide. He did not go looking for God to confess his sin. Rather, he hid himself. His once welcoming relationship with God was now interrupted.

To communicate effectively, we must be able to share an array of emotions. There are times when we will plead with God to listen—not because He is otherwise engaged but because we feel as though He is not listening. The book of Psalms is replete with such pleas. For example, "O Lord, God of my salvation, I have cried out day and night before You. Let my prayer come before You; incline Your ear to my cry" (Ps. 88:1, 2).

We can also present to Him our complaints. However, our complaints are more about us than they are about God. "God, you are not listening to me!" "God, why aren't you answering me?" "God, how long must I wait? I'm tired of asking and waiting." God has a timetable that is perfect. Were we to submit to God's purpose, we would not complain but only trust. However, complaining is not necessarily bad. It is a means of expressing emotions, and we can find complaints in the Psalms. "I cry out to the LORD with my voice; with my voice to the LORD I make my supplication. I pour out my complaint before Him; I declare before Him my trouble" (Ps. 142:1, 2). "LORD, I cry out to You; make haste to me! Give ear to my voice when I cry out to You" (Ps. 141:1).

God can handle our impatience, and He can also handle our requests. "And my God shall supply all your need according to His riches in glory by Christ Jesus" (Phil. 4:19). God is waiting for us to make our requests with thanksgiving. His promise suggests that He is more willing to give than we are to ask.

## Prayer, when entered into properly, makes us aware of the presence of God

Psalm 16:11 says: "You will show me the path of life; in Your presence is fullness of joy; at Your right hand are pleasures forevermore." Without the person, there is no presence. With what or with whom do you associate joy? What picture do you have of God? Our picture of God can deeply affect the way we experience God's presence. Whenever we speak to someone who we think is not listening, we feel frustrated and depersonalized.

Being aware of essential characteristics of God can be a powerful means of leading us into intentionality. Coming into the presence of God is intentional. This intentionality was displayed by David, "I have set the Lord always before me; because He is at my right hand I shall not be moved" (Ps. 16:8).

*The result of being in the presence of God is confidence— confidence born out of God's ability to protect, defend, and provide*

The result of being in the presence of God is confidence—confidence born out of God's ability to protect, defend, and provide.

## Prayer then allows us to face life void of anxiety

Do not be anxious about anything, but in every situation, by prayer and petition, with thanksgiving, present your requests to God. And the peace of God, which transcends all understanding, will guard your hearts and minds in Christ Jesus. (Phil. 4:6, 7, NIV)

David again declares in Psalm 23, "The LORD is my shepherd; I shall not want. He makes me lie down in green pastures, He restores my soul." The focus is on God and His ability, not on my own limitations.

If God is able and willing and if He is listening to us, then we need not be anxious. The strength of our relationship with Him allows us to express feelings and emotions that would otherwise be inappropriate and unacceptable. Certain feelings and emotions are not appropriate for a casual relationship, while in an intimate relationship they are absolutely appropriate.

## Prayer is focusing on who God is rather than on ourselves or our circumstances

Let's look at the example provided in the experience of Jehoshaphat, King of Judah. "O LORD God of our fathers, are You not God in heaven, and do You not rule over all the kingdoms of the nations, and in Your hand is there not power and might, so that no one is able to withstand You?" (2 Chron. 20:6). Jehoshaphat was open, honest, and constructive with the problem that confronted him. He knew Moab and Ammon were better prepared for war than he and his people, so he acknowledged that fact and did not stop there. He shifted his focus from his problem to the strength of his God. Though he and his people were no match for the enemy, their God was.

## Prayer is not so much getting answers from God as it is being with God

God will keep you in perfect peace when your mind stays upon Him, when you rest in Him. Jehoshaphat was told to relax because he was in the presence of the Almighty.

Do not be afraid nor dismayed because of this great multitude, for the battle is not yours, but God's.... You will not need to fight in this battle. Position yourselves, stand still and see the salvation of the LORD, who is with you, O Judah and Jerusalem! Do not fear or be dismayed; tomorrow go out against them, for the LORD is with you. (2 Chron. 20:15, 17)

The outcome was nothing short of spectacular. Yet, before they saw the result, they were praising God—a stellar reflection of their faith in God. Faith is "the substance of things hoped for, the evidence of things not seen" (Heb. 11:1). We walk by faith, not by sight.

## Prayer improves the quality of our relationship with God

Jehoshaphat was intentional about his relationship with God, and so were other Bible characters, as you should also be. Notice David's plea in Psalm 51:

"Do not cast me away from Your presence, and do not take Your Holy Spirit from me." (Ps. 51:11)

"Shout to God, all the earth! Sing out the honor of His name; make His praise glorious. Say to God 'How awesome are Your works! Through the greatness of Your power Your enemies shall submit themselves to You. All the earth shall worship You and sing praises to You; they shall sing praises to Your name.'" (Ps. 66:1–4).

Praise should be incorporated in our prayers, and, when we focus on God for who He is, we experience transformation in every area of our lives. And what are the results?

- Truthfulness
  "Behold, I was brought forth in iniquity, and in sin my mother conceived me. Behold, You desire truth in the inward parts, and in the hidden part You will make me to know wisdom" (Ps. 51:5, 6).
- Wisdom
- Awareness of God's presence and the worth of other human beings
- Purity

- The removal of guilt
- Joy
- Patience
- Gladness
- Humility
- Rejoicing
- The assurance of salvation (Ps. 51:7–13)

## Prayer opens up the channel for God's omnipotent power to flow to and through us

When rightly understood and used correctly, praise brings power to our prayers, and it directs us to the awareness that God is willing and able to answer our prayers.

> We have thought, O God, on Your lovingkindness, in the midst of Your temple. According to Your name, O God, so is Your praise to the ends of the earth; Your right hand is full of righteousness. Let Mount Zion rejoice, let the daughters of Judah be glad, because of Your judgments. Walk about Zion, and go all around her. Count her towers; mark well her bulwarks; consider her palaces; that you may tell it to the generation following. For this is God, our God forever and ever; He will be our guide even to death. (Ps. 48:9–14)

Reflect on some of the characteristics of God that can reinforce this concept of praying with a spirit of praise. God is:

- The Creator
- Omniscient
- Sovereign
- Gracious
- Almighty
- Kind
- Faithful.

When we work, *we* work. Yet, when we pray, *God* works. Prayer is the secret of spiritual power. It brings us into immediate contact with God and gives us spiritual strength.

Here are some ways in which God may choose to release His supernatural power over your life, when you pray with the spirit of praise:

- Wisdom
- An idea you desperately need
- Courage greater than you could muster on your own
- Confidence
- Perseverance
- Uncommon staying power
- A changed attitude
- Changed circumstances
- An outright miracle.

## Prayer allows us to plug into God's sustaining power

It is hard for God to release His power when we put our hands in our pockets and say, "I can handle it on my own." Prayerless people cut themselves off from God's supernatural power. Consequently, we have feelings of being:

- Overwhelmed
- Beaten down
- Pushed around
- Defeated
- Discouraged.

If you have not been in the habit of praying, don't panic. If willful sin is making you unwilling to pray, consider the closeness of the relationship that existed between God and David and between God and Peter. David was a deliberate adulterer and murderer, and Peter publicly denied that he knew Jesus shortly after he had pledged loyalty to Him. Why were these men such favorites of God? It is because they both deeply desired a close relationship with God. The direction of their lives was more important than their occasional misdeeds. What does the trajectory of your life look like? Is it moving in a God-ward direction? Is it strong enough to overcome the occasional misdeeds in your life? Pray, as David did when he cried out, "Have mercy upon me, O God, according to Your lovingkindness; according to the multitude of Your tender mercies, blot out my transgressions. Wash me thoroughly from my iniquity, and cleanse me from my sin" (Ps. 51:1, 2). Pray, as did Peter, when he remembered the word of Jesus and went out and wept bitterly. You, too, can do the same.

## Prayer is the key to unleashing God's supernatural power in our lives

If you are frustrated and feel like your efforts are not yielding the results you desire, stop working and start praying—and not the usual prayer saturated with "thank you" and "Lord, give me," but, rather, prayers bathed in the reality of who God is—a loving, caring, compassionate, transforming, and capable God, who stands alone in His uniqueness. "There is none like You, O God."

"Cast your burden on the LORD, and He shall sustain you; He shall never permit the righteous to be moved" (Ps. 55:22).

He is faithful.

"Now to Him who is able to do exceedingly abundantly above all that we ask or think, according to the power that works in us" (Eph. 3:20).

God wants to hear from you. He is ready and willing to listen.

"It shall come to pass that before they call, I will answer; and while they are still speaking, I will hear" (Isa. 65:24).

Focus right now on the wisdom of God and the love of God. There is no one wiser or more loving than He.

## Prayer is asking God to transform you into the person that He, in His sovereign will, wants you to be

Romans 12:2 says: "And do not be conformed to this world, but be transformed by the renewing of your mind, that you may prove what is that good and acceptable and perfect will of God." God's will for your life is good, acceptable, and perfect. Don't you think it is worth it to search out His will and give it your all?

*We* live in time; *God* exists in eternity. Our Maker has a purpose for our creation. Let's find that purpose and pursue it with all the energy we can muster. Victory is assured. "Yet in all these things we are more than conquerors through Him who loved us" (Rom. 8:37). Based on the merits of His Son Jesus

Christ, we who have failed so many times—we who have been beaten up by the enemy—are, in the eyes of God, more than conquerors.

## Chapter 2

# TO WHOM DO WE PRAY?

Human beings enjoy knowing the one with whom they have a relationship. God is not unmindful of our need to know Him, so He provides us with a divine self-revelation. That is, whatever we know about God is what God wants us to know about Him. Job is probably the oldest book of the Bible, and its author asks the question, "Canst thou by searching find out God? canst thou find out the Almighty unto perfection?" (Job 11:7, KJV). The obvious answer is: No, we cannot. If we could know everything that there is to know about God, it would make God less than who He is. In fact, He would cease to be God, for He would no longer be the Infinite One.

> *If we could know everything that there is to know about God, it would make God less than who He is. In fact, He would cease to be God, for He would no longer be the Infinite One*

Moses, when he was being commissioned to go back to Egypt to request the release of the Israelites, made this request:

> Then Moses said to God, "Indeed when I come to the children of Israel and say to them, the God of your fathers has sent me to you, and they say to me, 'What is His name?' What should I say to them?" And God said to Moses, "I AM WHO I AM."

And he said, "Thus shall you say to the children of Israel, 'I AM has sent me to you.'" Moreover God said to Moses, "Thus you shall say to the children of Israel: 'The Lord God of your fathers, the God of Abraham, the God of Isaac, and the God of Jacob, has sent me to you. This is My name forever, and this is My memorial to all generations.'" (Exod. 3:13–15).

God reveals Himself relationally. Yet, He is not a new God; He is the God of their ancestors. He is from everlasting to everlasting. There is no hesitation on God's part in revealing His identity to His people. After He fulfilled His promise to release Israel from Egyptian bondage, He expanded on the early revelation of Himself (Exod. 3:13–15) with more detail:

Now the LORD descended in the cloud and stood with him there and proclaimed the name of the LORD. And the Lord passed before him and proclaimed, "The LORD, the LORD God, merciful and gracious, longsuffering, and abounding in goodness and truth, keeping mercy for thousands, forgiving iniquity and transgression and sin, by no means clearing the guilty, visiting the iniquity of the fathers upon the children and the children's children to the third and the fourth generation." (Exod. 34:5–7)

It is very clear that God is willing to reveal Himself to us because He wants a personal relationship with us. We can therefore conclude that God is willing and ever present. He is a loving, caring, capable, giving God who is never too busy to listen to His children.

In Luke 18:1–5, Jesus tells the story of the experience of a widow who was quite likely uneducated, jobless, and poor, having no property, power, or status. She knew that she was entitled to justice even though the judge she petitioned had the reputation of being unjust. The widow called upon him relentlessly, and, as a result, the unjust judge ruled in her favor. Jesus had prefaced the story with the words: "That men always ought to pray and not lose heart." In other words, don't give up. God is more willing to grant your request than an unrelenting, unjust judge. If this widow was willing to throw herself on the mercy of an unjust judge who did not fear God or His justice, should we not be more enthused to go to our heavenly Father who is the embodiment of love and justice?

Justice sometimes comes only through persistence, and God is worth waiting on. If, while we are waiting on Him, we run out of strength, He will renew our strength. God is not like the unjust judge. The story is a study in contrasts. For one thing, we are not like the widow: We are God's children. We have status with God. Everything that we need, God has already made provision to supply. We do not need to be fearful about approaching God because He thinks about us even when we are not thinking about Him.

For another thing, our heavenly Father is not like the unjust judge. He introduces Himself to us and our ancestors as "merciful and gracious, longsuffering, and abounding in goodness and truth, ... forgiving iniquity and transgression and sin" (Exod. 34:6, 7). This warms my spirit and makes me want to experience and display these essentials of our God's character. Is it any wonder that the psalmist David exclaimed: "Oh, taste and see that the LORD is good!" (Ps. 34:8).

> **We do not need to be fearful about approaching God because He thinks about us even when we are not thinking about Him**

Indeed, God is good. He waits for us to come to Him, not timidly, but boldly. Thank God that this boldness is not based on our performance but on what Jesus has done. Look how the writer of Hebrews assures us:

> Seeing then that we have a great High Priest who has passed through the heavens, Jesus the Son of God, let us hold fast our confession. For we do not have a High Priest who cannot sympathize with our weaknesses, but was in all points tempted as we are, yet without sin. Let us therefore come boldly to the throne of grace, that we may obtain mercy and find grace to help in time of need" (Heb. 4:14–16).

God loves to bestow blessings on His children. Why is that? It is because it is His nature. He is a giving God, a blessing God, an encouraging God, a nurturing God, an empowering God, and a loving God. We cannot begin to fully comprehend all that there is of God.

God gives lavishly. God is looking for opportunities to pour out His blessings on us. Since He is the giver of all blessings, He challenges us to return to Him a tenth of what we have already received from Him and see if He will not open the windows of heaven and pour out for us "such blessing that there will not be room enough to receive it" (Mal. 3:10). God will bless the crops of His obedient children (Lev. 26:3-6). He said that the blessings would overtake them if they obeyed (Deut. 28:2-6, 12). God's blessings will likewise overtake us if we obey.

We are adopted into God's family, on the basis of Jesus' good pleasure (Eph. 1:5). It is an accomplished fact that changes our status from slaves to sons (Gal. 4:7; Rom. 8:16, 17). Jesus taught us to call God our Father (Matt. 6:9).

The God to whom we pray wants to shower us with blessings because we are His children and because He is madly in love with us. He is a generous Father who is more willing to give good gifts to us when we ask than an earthly father is willing to give good gifts to his children (Matt. 7:9-11). He waits for us to accept His gifts.

## God is able

It is one thing to want to do something, it is quite another to be able to do it. However, God is not only willing, but He is able. Consider how Paul speaks about God's ability: "Now to Him who is able to do exceedingly abundantly above all that we ask or think, according to the power that works in us, to Him be glory in the church by Christ Jesus to all generations, forever and ever. Amen" (Eph. 3:20, 21). If you could ask God for one thing, what would it be? Be mindful of His ability. He is able to do exceeding abundantly above all that you can ask or think. He has no limit within Himself or within the universe. Go ahead and think your finest thought, and know that you are dealing with a God who has no limit to His ability.

Now think about your circumstances and problems. Do you really believe that God can handle them? Many of us have deep problems, but we refuse to bring them to God because deep down we don't believe God can or will do anything about them, or because, we wonder, if He should act, will it be what we want? So we choose to live with our problems. Nevertheless, we should never forget that God is waiting for us to recognize His power and ask for His help.

The God to whom we pray wants us to know that, in the midst of mounting problems, we can focus on God's omnipotence, rather than the size of the problem. To focus on our problem is to get on a self-defeating track that will only lead to greater frustration. In order to overcome this self-defeating belief, we must humbly confess our unbelief in God's omnipotence. Jesus confronted the problem of unbelief with a parent who was desperately seeking help and, at the same time, confessing his unbelief. Look at the man's desperate plea and Jesus' response in Mark's account of the encounter. "But if You can do anything, have compassion on us and help us." Jesus said to him, "If you can believe, all things are possible to him who believes." Immediately the father of the child cried out and said with tears, "Lord, I believe; help my unbelief!" (Mark 9:22–24).

Jesus redirected the father's focus in a very subtle way through His response to the man's plea. He said, in effect: Don't question my ability; rather, recognize your inability. Your ability is hampered by your unbelief, something I don't ever have to be concerned with. I'm fully secure in who I am, and I am always ready to give you assistance. Do you believe that I can do what you are asking of me? Do you believe that your son can be healed? Do you still believe that even after others who are in association with me have failed, that I can fulfill your request? These are questions that we too must reflect on because, even when they don't rise to the surface, they still lie buried beneath, and they eat away at us.

The Bible reminds us that God has power over nature. He parted seas and rivers (Exod. 14; Joshua 3). He dropped food from heaven and multiplied bread and fish to satisfy His hungry children (Exod. 16; John 6:1–13). He stilled the storm (Mark 4:35–41). He extended daylight in response to Joshua's bold declarations as Joshua sought revenge on the enemies of God's people (Joshua

10:12–14); He brought water out of a rock to quench the thirst of man and beast (Exod. 17:1–7).

In our day, with the ever-increasing frequency of natural disasters, we can be comforted in the knowledge that God has power over nature. Are you a survivor of a natural disaster? Tell your story. Give God praise and honor.

God has power over our circumstances. Peter was in prison, and the church engaged in constant prayer for him. They had great difficulty acknowledging God's quick response to their prayer.

Yes, God's response to our less-than-perfect faith does astonish us (Acts 12:7–12). However, it is reassuring to me—and I hope to you as well—that God blessed the incomplete faith of His children.

The God to whom we pray has power not only over nature and circumstance, but He has control over our lives, and He has power to change people's lives. He made timid Moses a bold leader (Exod. 11:1–8). He kept a discouraged Elijah from quitting (1 Kings 19:15–18). He transformed a Christian-hating Saul into the amazing Christ-loving Apostle Paul (Acts 9:1–31) and a self-seeking Peter into a selfless Peter (Luke 22:31, 32; John 21:15–19). Is there any hope for us? Oh, yes there is! Paul tells us that the work of reconciliation is still effective today, and he concludes with these words, "Therefore, if anyone is in Christ, he is a new creation; old things have passed away; behold, all things have become new" (2 Cor. 5:17).

The God who did all this is and who continues to change lives today is the same yesterday, today, and forevermore (Heb. 13:8).

The God to whom we pray is immutable. "Immutable" means that He does not change. "For I am the LORD, I do not change" (Mal. 3:6). Jesus Christ is "the same yesterday, today and forevermore" (Heb. 13:8). God asks: "Have you not known? Have you not heard? The everlasting God, the LORD, the Creator of the ends of the earth, neither faints nor is weary, His understanding is unsearchable. He gives power to the weak, and to those who have no might He increases strength" (Isa. 40:28, 29).

Have you ever been in a situation in which you were depending on someone who—in the past—had shown himself or herself unreliable? It is quite an unsettling experience, isn't it? I am so grateful that God can be trusted, based on His word and character.

Today, I'm more convinced than ever that the single most important thing that we can say about God is that *He is able*—able to save in times of deep distress. When no one else can reach us to help, God is there. Scripture gives us overwhelming evidence of God's ability. Here are a few such examples. He was able to save the three Hebrew boys from fire (Dan. 3:17). He was able to save Daniel from hungry lions (Dan. 6:20–22). He was able to make the 90-year-old postmenopausal and barren Sarah have a baby (Gen. 18:13, 14; 21:1, 2; Rom. 4:18–21). He is able to give His children all they need so that they can have all sufficiency in all things (2 Cor. 9:8). He is able to save completely those who come to Him (Heb. 7:25). Yes, God is able to do much more than we can ask or think (Eph. 3:20).

I hope that you are as convinced as I am about God's ability. I know that I can rest confidently in His care, and I have no fear when I respond to His glorious invitation.

## God's Invitation

Yes, He invites us to pray continually (1 Thess. 5:17). Come confidently to Me, He says, and I will give you rest (Matt. 11:28, 29). Don't be anxious; just let your request be known to Me (Phil. 4:6). I am ready to respond.

Wherever you are praying, lift up holy hands (1 Tim. 2:8). Pray with confidence; be bold (Heb. 4:16) because God loves you with an everlasting love. Even when things are not going the way you would like them to go, you must remember who is in control and that a loving Father waits to hear from you (John 16:26, 27).

Don't be foolish. Accept His invitation (James 4:2, 7, 8), and, when you accept the invitation and start praying, miracles will occur in your relationships, family, career, ministry, witnessing, and finances. As long as you are convinced that God is willing and able and that He has invited you to come to Him in prayer, miracles will happen.

God is so confident in His position, ability, and willingness as the Sovereign of the universe that He says, "before you call I will answer and while you are still speaking I will hear" (Isa. 65:24, paraphrased). How awesome is our God! I am grateful for who God is and how He relates to us.

## Chapter 3

# A PERFECT PRAYER PATTERN

Thinking back, I remember my sister-in-law making many dresses from patterns. Whenever we are not sure how to do something, it is a great advantage to have a pattern. When it comes to prayer, there are many patterns. Two of the better-known patterns are **ABC**, ask-believe-claim, and **ACTS**, adoration-confession-thanksgiving-supplication. I prefer the second pattern because the first seems to make God out to be less than He really is. God is more than just someone we go to when we need something. God is autonomous. He is not answerable to anyone else. While God recognizes and honors our faith in Him, faith alone cannot accomplish anything. Faith needs a power source, and not just *any* power source but an *endless* power source, an endless power source that is controlled by someone who has perfect knowledge of the past, present, and future. That someone is God. He is omniscient, omnipresent, omnipotent, faithful, and loving.

> *If God were to answer all our prayers, we would be completely destroyed, because we do not know what to ask for*

Most of our prayers are saturated with "Please give me ... help me ... and thank You." When this is our pattern, it places *us* in control and reduces God to someone who simply carries out orders. If God were to answer all our prayers, we would be completely destroyed, because we do not know what to ask for. Knowing this, God gives us the ministry of the Holy Spirit who makes intercession for us with groanings that cannot be uttered (Rom. 8:26).

ACTS—adoration, confession, thanksgiving, and supplication—allows us to keep the focus where it truly belongs—on God. So let's get started.

## Adoration

Adoration is worship at its best. It shines the light on God and keeps it there. There are many reasons we should begin our prayers with adoration, but, for our purposes, we will focus on just four.

First, adoration centers the entire prayer on God and not on us. It reminds us that we are in the presence of the Alpha and the Omega—the all-powerful, all-knowing, eternal God.

Second, adoration forces us to reflect on God's identity and what He can do. Think about just this one attribute of God—His omnipresence. Whether I am in an airplane or in a car, God is always there, and, therefore, I need not ask Him to come but instead to make me aware of His presence. When I leave my family and friends behind, God does not have to abandon me in order to be with them. Awesome, isn't it?

Third, adoration empties my mind of thoughts about myself. In other words, adoration purges me of selfish thoughts. My sense of desperation is replaced with thoughts of God's greatness. It enables me to enjoy God for who He is.

Fourth, adoration reminds me of God's worth. He is worthy of all praise. God has bestowed such great love on us that we can be called His children (1 John 3:1). So, the very beginning of our prayers should focus not on who we are or on our needs but on the awesomeness of God, who is worthy of all our praise. We can learn from David when he declared: "I will bless the LORD at all times; His praise shall continually be in my mouth" (Ps. 34:1).

How then do we worship or adore God? We adore God by focusing on who He is. We take His attributes and praise Him for each one. When I find myself feeling inadequate, I praise Him for His sufficiency. When I am weak, I praise Him for His strength. When I am feeling foolish, I praise Him for His wisdom.

## Confession

We are woefully lacking where confession is concerned. We use catchall phrases like, "Please forgive us for all our sins." When we ask for forgiveness, we need to name our sins—not for God's benefit, but for our own. We need to confront our sins, or else they will always have dominion over us. If I have been in a situation where I acted selfishly, I need to say, "Lord, forgive me for acting selfishly today when I took the parking space that that other driver was waiting on." Sin is not determined by things others would not do. Sin is breaking God's law. It is missing the standard that God has set for us to live by.

Confession has certain advantages. It allows us to be honest with God. It clears the conscience. As Paul declared, he had a conscience void of offense toward God and man (Acts 24:16). Confession assures us of God's forgiveness. His word is absolutely true, "If we confess our sins, He is faithful and just to forgive us our sins and cleanse us from all unrighteousness" (1 John 1:9). We should think of the distance between the east and the west and be mindful that that is how far God removes our sins from us (Ps. 103:12).

With this assurance, we can feel free to pray for power to forsake sin. When we take confession seriously, we break the stranglehold of sin and begin to experience change towards newness of life (2 Cor. 5:17).

## Thanksgiving

An accompanying phenomenon of thanksgiving is joy. Thanksgiving allows us to focus on divine acts in our past—what God has done because of who He is. David reminds us that we should not forget God's benefits toward us (Ps. 103:2). Paul says that we are to give thanks in all circumstances (1 Thess. 5:18). In God's presence is fullness of joy and at His right hand are pleasures forevermore (Ps. 16:11). How awesome is our God!

God blesses us in four areas, and we need to thank Him for those blessings. These are:

- Answered prayers
- Spiritual blessings
- Relational blessings
- Material blessings.

When Jesus healed the ten lepers, only one returned to give Jesus thanks, and that leper was a foreigner! Through this miracle, Jesus wanted to remind us who are His children not to take His blessings for granted. We are not to harbor the spirit of entitlement, but the spirit of thankfulness. God's answer to our prayer obligates us to thank Him. We, in response to His blessings, should give Him praise.

## Supplication

Supplication challenges us to focus on others, to think about the needs of others and, in so doing, we are ultimately blessed with a quiet and peaceable life. "Therefore I exhort first of all that supplications, prayers, intercessions, and giving of thanks be made for all men, for kings and all who are in authority, that we may lead a quiet and peaceable life in all godliness and reverence" (1 Tim. 2:1, 2).

Nothing is too big or too small for God to handle. When it comes to supplication, we are to be mindful that we do not have all the information, so we are to be honest with God. Let Him know that we are not sure and that we are surrendering our requests to His perfect knowledge of the past, present, and future. We can make requests in every area of our lives—in our vocation, in our family, in our relationships with people, and in our personal and spiritual needs. In each of these areas, we are to be specific. Refrain from making blanket requests like: "Lord, please bless me today, bless my family and my friends."

At the conclusion of our prayers, we should feel lighter, with an unburdened kind of carefree feeling, because we have followed

His instructions in casting all our cares upon Him because He cares for us (1 Peter 5:7). In my time of need, I am not afraid to go to God because He invites me to "come boldly to the throne of grace that I may obtain mercy and find grace to help in times of need" (Heb. 4:16, paraphrased).

Be practical. If you have difficulty staying on task with your prayer, write it out, and then read it to God. And not only that, at regular intervals go back and review your written prayers, and make a note of the answers that God has granted. It will prove to be a faith-building experience. If this simple pattern does not work for you, find one that does and work that pattern. Your loving heavenly Father is waiting to hear from you. Be careful not to keep the King of heaven waiting too long.

## Chapter 4

# PRAYER AND FAITH

I tell you the truth, if you have faith and do not doubt... You will be able to say to this mountain, 'Go, fall into the sea.' And if you have faith, it will happen" (Matt. 21:21, NCV).

Though it is the authentic word of Jesus, the above statement was said over two thousand years ago, and I have not seen any mountains moved. So you need to get your head screwed on right and stop looking for literal mountains to move. God has better things to do than to excavate mountains and dump them into the sea. Jesus was using the term "mountain" figuratively.

Whatever obstacle stands in your way, whatever difficulty impedes your progress, that is your "mountain," and God can move it, when you pray the prayer of faith. How do we develop mountain-moving faith? In order to get the desired effect, here are three simple things to remember.

### Focus on God, not your problem

God has given everyone a measure of faith. "Faith comes by hearing, and hearing by the word of God." (Rom. 10:17). When we focus on God, we do better than when we focus on the problem. It's amazing how things change when we change our focus. Moses looked at the mistreatment of his fellow Hebrews in Egypt and took matters into his own hands, and, as a result, he spent the next forty years in the land of Midian feeding sheep. When I focus on myself, I will always be overwhelmed. I will mess up. I will feel grossly inadequate. But, God is always able to do exceedingly, abundantly above all that I am able to ask or think.

God is almighty, all wise, and, if He runs out of resources, He can make some more. God is always faithful, always kind, always compassionate, always loving, always holy, and always righteous, irrespective of who I am or what I have done.

When we focus on God rather than on our problem, we see changes that we would not otherwise see.

Jehoshaphat refused to look solely at the problem but focused on God as a Father, Creator, ruler over all kingdoms, and as the all-powerful, Almighty God who defends His people. "O our God, will You not judge them? For we have no power against this great multitude that is coming against us; nor do we know what to do, but our eyes are upon You" (2 Chron. 20:12).

## Walk in obedience

Every good and perfect gift comes from above. God gives us faith as we walk in obedience to Him (James 1:17). The Bible gives us many examples of this kind of faith.

Joshua 3 illustrates the prayer of faith. After spending forty years in the wilderness, Israel is now on the banks of the Jordan River, the only thing standing between them and the Promised Land. The river is impassable, turbulent, and deep. Have you been there before? You can see the thing that you have waited for, worked for, dreamed of, and finally, there is an obstacle impeding your progress. You are frustrated, fed up, and out of options. But then you remember God, and God does not do what you think He would do.

God could build a bridge right before their eyes, or dry up the waters, but not this time. Moses is dead, and the miracle of the parting of the Red Sea is a distant memory. God does not do anything like He did in their history, nor does He do the obvious. They are thinking about the fertile land beyond the river, but their eyes are on the river. And they wonder, *How are we going to cross over?* In the midst of their perplexity, God gives Joshua specific directives to the people to pass on over. They are to keep their eyes on the ark, the visible symbol of the invisible God, carried by the priests, and they are to fall in line behind the priests at a proscribed distance.

## Command the priests bearing the ark to stand in the midst of the river

We must never underestimate the power of God. Remember, God is not subject to human logic. He is the Creator of all laws. He understands them perfectly and is not limited by them. Obedience to God requires courage and a willingness to break with tradition and to go against even what we know to be proven laws. The priests obeyed, and, as a result, this is what happened.

> "Now the Jordan is at flood stage all during harvest. Yet as soon as the priest who carried the ark reached the Jordan and their feet touched the water's edge, the water from upstream stopped flowing. It piled up in a heap at great distance away, at a town called Adam in the vicinity of Zarethan, while the water flowing down to the Sea of the Arabah (that is, the Dead Sea) was completely cut off. So the people crossed over opposite Jericho. The priests who carried the ark of the covenant of the LORD stopped in the middle of the Jordan and stood on dry ground, while all Israel passed by until the whole nation had completed the crossing on dry ground" (Joshua 3:15–17, NIV).

God did not give Joshua or the priests evidence that the water would part. Nothing happened until they acted. Only then did God act by stopping the flow of the river. Could it be that your refusal to walk in obedience is keeping your mountain in place? Your mountain will move only when you obey. What mountain are you facing right now? Take the first step. Keep your eyes on God, not on your problem. Obey, move forward, and your mountain will move over. Obedience is not legalism. It is your expression of love to God for what He has done for you.

When we shift our focus from our problem to our God, mountains will move. As we walk in obedience to God, our faith will grow. Our confidence will increase, and our prayers will have power.

## Expect something great to happen

Twelve spies looked over the land; ten thought conquering it was impossible, and just two said that it was possible. Ten saw the giants; two saw the all-powerful God of Israel. They declared, "The faithful God who promised us the land will give it to us!" What are you focusing on right now? Do you see your insufficiency instead of God's sufficiency? (Num. 13). People who expect something great to happen, pray with enthusiasm and passion and pay attention to ways in which God might act to answer their prayers.

## 1 Samuel 17—David and Goliath

Saul and his army saw a giant that they could not defeat, and they were terrified. David saw a God who could not be defeated, and he said, "My God is able. Let me go." People who expect something great to happen when they pray, pray more because they have had answers, and they know that chances of finding answers through other sources are relatively slim. These individuals are more likely to invite others to pray because they have experienced great results and are enthusiastic about what God has done. They take greater interest in mentoring others in the habit of praying.

*Stop telling God about your problem, and start telling your problem about your God*

Are you standing in the shadow of a mountain right now? What is that mountain? Is it a destructive habit, a financial problem, a physical disability, or a relationship on the rocks? Have you stood so long in its shadow that you have gotten accustomed to it? Shift the focus of your prayer. Stop telling God about your problem, and start telling your problem about your God. God knows more about your problem than you do. Start walking in obedience and watch your mountain move. Expect God to do the impossible. He opened deaf ears. He opened blind eyes. He cleansed the leper. He raised the dead. He fed five thousand with a little boy's lunch. He brought water out of a rock. He saved you, which took a miracle of love and grace.

## CHAPTER 5

# UNHINDERED PRAYER

Much has been said about prayer and its importance to the Christian. In fact, Ellen White indicates that: "Prayer is the breath of the soul. It is the secret of spiritual power. No other means of grace can be substituted and the health of the soul be preserved. Prayer brings the heart into immediate contact with the Wellspring of life, and strengthens the sinew and muscle of the religious experience" (*Prayer,* p. 12). If indeed prayer is "the breath of the soul" and the secret of spiritual power, then every effort should be made to keep the spiritual airways open because the wellbeing of the soul depends upon it. "Husbands, likewise, dwell with them with understanding, giving honor to the wife, as to the weaker vessel, and as being heirs together of the grace of life, that your prayers may be not hindered" (1 Peter 3:7).

If husbands refuse to see their wives as needing to be understood, honored, and treated as the weaker partner, as well as being equally in need of God's grace as they themselves, their prayers will be hindered or not even be answered. Thinking about how this is, I became curious. If this is true for husbands in relation to their wives, might there be other things that could prevent other people besides husbands from having their prayers answered? And if this is so, what might those things be?

As I read 2 Chronicles 7:12–15, it provided me with a platform on which to apply this to all Christians. Here are the words of God: "I have heard your prayer, and have chosen this place for

Myself as a house of sacrifice. When I shut up heaven and there is no rain, or command the locusts to devour the land, or send pestilence among My people, if My people who are called by My name will humble themselves, and pray and seek My face; and turn from their wicked ways, then I will hear from heaven, and will forgive their sin and heal their land. Now My eyes will be open and My ears attentive to prayer made in this place."

These verses contain good news and bad news. The good news is that God does not disown wayward people. The bad news is that people who are proud and refuse to pray will not come into God's presence and repent of their evil deeds and that they will, therefore, not have their prayers answered.

David made it personal when he wrote: "If I regard iniquity in my heart, the Lord will not hear" (Psalm 66:18). However, Isaiah applies this truth in a general way as he maintains God's assurance not to disown His people. "Behold, the LORD's hand is not shortened, that it cannot save; nor His ears heavy, that it cannot hear. But your iniquities have separated you from your God; and your sins have hidden His face from you, so that He will not hear. For your hands are defiled with blood, and your fingers with iniquity; your lips have spoken lies, Your tongue has muttered perversity" (Isa. 59:1–3).

The Bible is very clear—God has the ability to forgive sins and to blot out iniquities. However, in order for Him to forgive sins, we must do our part. David pleads: "Direct my steps by Your word, and let no iniquity have dominion over me" (Ps. 119:133). Isaiah declares, "All we like sheep have gone astray; we have turned, every one, to his own way; and the LORD has laid on Him the iniquity of us all" (Isa. 53:6). God laid on Jesus all our iniquity. Micah wrote:

> Who is a God like You, pardoning iniquity and passing over the transgression of the remnant of His heritage? He does not retain His anger forever, because He delights in mercy. He will again have compassion on us, and will subdue our iniquities. You will cast all our sins into the depths of the sea. (Micah 7:18, 19)

Is it any wonder that Micah would follow this penetrating and awe-inspiring question with an equally awe-inspiring answer? God is the answer to the problem of sin. He laid our sins on His Son, and He will not only have compassion on us, but He will subdue our iniquities. God will wrestle our sins to the ground, wrap them up in a bundle, and cast them into the depths of the sea.

## How should we approach God to reap the benefits of unhindered prayer?

Here are four qualities that we need to exhibit if our prayers are to be unhindered: integrity, commitment, humility, and a willingness to learn. In 2 Chronicles 7:14, we see God's call to His people to live lives of integrity, void of hypocrisy, and, in humility, to seek God's face and turn away from wickedness. If our sins separate us from our God, we cannot expect to get our prayers answered. If you are not sure, don't give up. There is a way out of the seemingly unending maze.

The first prerequisite for unhindered prayer is, therefore, integrity. Integrity requires that what we are on the inside should be consistent with what we are on the outside. Integrity requires that we lay aside the sins that trip us up by admitting, confessing, and forsaking them in humility by God's help. Sin, as Peter has said, hinders our prayers. So, in whatever form sin persists in our lives, we must seek divine aid to rid ourselves of it, knowing, as Ellen White wrote:

> Every sincere prayer is heard in heaven. It may not be fluently expressed; but if the heart is in it, it will ascend to the sanctuary where Jesus ministers, and He will present it to the Father without one awkward, stammering word, beautiful and fragrant with the incense of His own perfection. (*The Desire of Ages,* p. 667)

The very fact that God does not disown us as a result of the presence of sin in our lives and that Jesus presents us to His Father with the incense of His own perfection assures us that He will be available to forgive our sins when we confess them. "If we confess our sins, He is faithful and just to forgive us our sins and to cleanse us from all unrighteousness" (1 John 1:9). On the cross, Jesus offered "objective forgiveness" in the words: "Father, forgive them, for they do not know what they do" (Luke 23:34). Forgiveness is made available to people who are willing to live a life of integrity. Integrity, in and of itself, suggests overcoming obstruction and difficulty; and it is through the faithful striving of the heart and through prayer that we will arrive at the place of genuine spiritual health.

We are all shaken when we hear that someone in the religious or political world has fallen from grace. However, their fall did not happen overnight. It came as a result of little indiscretions over time. And, while the reasons for the fall could be many, that they have fallen points to one thing—a lack of integrity. Integrity is doing what is right even when no one is looking. The three Hebrew boys were persons of integrity. They could easily have compromised by pretending outwardly that they were worshiping the image, while protesting in their hearts. They could have reasoned that they were conforming so that their lives would be spared and they could go on to witness for God. As a result of their integrity, Nebuchadnezzar was forced to acknowledge that the fourth person in the fire was the Son of God.

When we pray, we must be mindful that we pray to a God who knows everything and cannot be deceived by us. God is omniscient. God knows our thoughts even before we are aware of them. He who created the world still watches over it and sustains it. Nothing in all of His creation is hidden from His view. He is aware of us as individuals. He knows our needs, the details of our lives, and our thoughts and motives. While others might have to conjecture, He knows without a shadow of a doubt. So prayer should not be considered simply an effort of our own. It is God's gift of grace to the sinner, and, when used in sincerity with integrity, it opens to us the resources of heaven.

But what good is it if the God that we serve knows everything and has no power to do anything about it? The Bible makes it clear that, not only does God know everything, but He also has all power. He is omnipotent! He can handle all our issues. There is nothing too small or too big for God to handle. King Jehoshaphat of Judah was well aware of God's ability, hence his question in 2 Chronicles 20:6: "O LORD God of our fathers, are You not God in heaven, and do You not rule over all the kingdoms of the nations, and in Your hand is there not power and might, so that no one is able to withstand You?"

Yes, God knows everything, and He has all power, but is He available whenever we need Him? Certainly, He does—because He is omnipresent. He is equally present everywhere. So, when I need Him in the United States and someone else needs Him in Africa, He doesn't have to leave me to take care of the problem over there. Ellen White remarked, "The relations between God and each soul are as distinct and full as though there were not another soul upon the earth to share His watchcare, not another soul for whom He gave His beloved Son" (*Steps to Christ,* p. 100). David further assures us, in Psalm 139, that wherever we are—even if we make our bed in hell—God is there. God can be counted on. He never changes. He is "the same yesterday, today, and forever" (Heb. 13:8). These characteristics of God let us know that He can be trusted. He is reliable. He is loving and available. He has integrity.

Integrity not only makes demands of us, but it also has its benefits. Integrity reduces stress and all the ill effects of stress. When our private lives are out of harmony with our public lives, we expend an inordinate amount of energy trying to protect ourselves from exposure and the embarrassment it will cause. Integrity gives us the freedom to live life joyfully. It increases our energy levels and makes us more productive.

Integrity is the first key to unhindered prayer, and it is not something that is developed overnight. Rather, it is the result of strict adherence to that which is right over a long period of time.

The second prerequisite to unhindered prayer is commitment. Finishing high school, earning a college degree, completing a project, holding down a job, maintaining a relationship—all these require commitment. Unhindered prayer also requires commitment. Commitment to a life of prayer changes everything; it allows us to see life and its challenges in a different light. In fact, angels will be by our side to give us strength and guidance in our hour of need. As the writer of Hebrews points out, "Are they not all ministering spirits sent forth to minister for those who will inherit salvation?" (Heb. 1:14).

In the Sermon on the Mount, Jesus counsels His hearers to ask, and it will be given to them. Such prayer is built on the concept of commitment. It means that, when you ask and keep on asking, you will receive. Commitment to a life of prayer suggests that other things will not preempt it and that we truly believe in the faithfulness of God. People who are committed to keeping the spiritual airways open will spend quality time in communication with God so that they can experience unhindered prayer. As it is in the physical life, where breathing is not under the conscious control of the will, so should it be in the spiritual life—prayer should come naturally. Amid the noise of life, we can breathe a prayer and heaven will hear. Paul counsels us to "pray without ceasing" (1 Thess. 5:17). Our commitment to prayer should not take second place to anything. It is in the secret chamber of prayer that we unleash the power of God over our lives. If we truly believe that God is the source of all power, why would we want to separate ourselves from Him? Commitment to anything or anyone takes time, and, when we commit, it changes our priorities and it changes us.

It does not take much commitment to sit and watch a football game or even to sit through a spirited worship service listening to a gifted speaker. However, if we wish to make a lasting change in our lives or to do something that will make a difference in the world, it takes commitment. Prayer, when used appropriately, allows us to tap into the power needed to build strong family relations, experience personal maturity, make changes in the community, and produce things that enrich the lives of others.

Without commitment to prayer, we run the risk of taking the credit for life's accomplishments, and we forget that it is God "who gives" us "power to get wealth" (Deut. 8:18) and who holds our very breath. Commitment is a strong, abiding belief in someone or something. Commitment allows us to stand firm for our convictions and to pursue our goals without wavering when the going gets tough. Like the Apostle Paul, we are at the place that we are willing to forget the things that are behind and reach for those that are ahead, pressing forward. What this means is that, as we commit to praying, we give up some of our freedom and independence, some of the things that we would otherwise want to do. Commitment allows us to put blinders on so we can focus on the matter at hand. Have you ever had the experience of your mind wandering off in the midst of prayer? Rather than seeing it as a distraction, make it a part of your prayer. Follow the trail, and see where it leads. God might just be seeking to get you to a different place, a place of His own choosing. It can be risky, but the rewards can also be very great.

I challenge you to commit to prayer today. Don't allow anything to squeeze it out of your schedule. The rewards are out of this world! Daniel reaped the rewards of a life committed to formally praying to God three times a day. When thrown into the lion's den, he was protected by the divine. God sent His angel to shut the lions' mouths so that there was no harm to Daniel. His enemies knew that he was committed to his God. They knew his time and place of prayer, so it was not difficult for them to catch him in the act. Darius, the king, was also aware of Daniel's commitment to his God, as evidenced in his question, "Daniel, servant of the living God, has your God, whom you serve continually, been able to deliver you from the lions?" (Dan. 6:20).

> *I challenge you to commit to prayer today. Don't allow anything to squeeze it out of your schedule. The rewards are out of this world*

Daniel did not just pray when it was safe or convenient. He prayed at all times. Like Daniel, are you committed to a life of prayer? Do you have a firm commitment to prayer? God honors those who are committed to prayer, and He will always reward them. Paul and Silas could have complained about God's failure to protect them while they were preaching the gospel in Philippi, but they took the beating instead. At midnight, they prayed and sang, and the angel of the Lord showed up and delivered them, saving the jailor and his family in the process. Our commitment is not just to prayer, it is a commitment to the God to whom we pray. He makes all the difference in the world. He is unstoppable. He can and will make a way where there is no way. Jesus reminds His followers: "If you abide in Me, and My words abide in you, you will ask what you desire, and it shall be done for you" (John 15:7).

The third prerequisite for unhindered prayer is humility. It is significant that, in 2 Chronicles 7:14, the first requirement mentioned is humility, and it is associated with prayer. Human beings are prone to be self-reliant. We pride ourselves in being able to pull ourselves up by our own bootstraps. It is the Nebuchadnezzar complex—"Is not this great Babylon, that I have built for a royal dwelling by my mighty power and for the honor of my majesty?" (Dan. 4:30). We are taught in the world to look out for number one, to go out and get whatever it is that we want, and to take the credit for our own success. However, humility allows us to keep life in proper balance, and it recognizes God as the eternal source, as our Senior Partner. Humility acknowledges that we cannot get along without the resources that our Senior Partner brings to the partnership.

Jesus warns us about the ugly effects of pride. He said that the Pharisees like the high seats at the feasts (Mark 12:39), but His followers are to take the low seat and wait to be called to a higher one. Jesus further counsels us not to pray like the hypocrites, which is to be seen by men, but, rather, we are to go into our closets, and our Father who sees in secret will reward us openly.

In 1 Peter 5:5, we have these words: "God resists the proud, but gives grace to the humble." Who would want to be resisted by the Almighty? I'm excited about what comes in verses 6 and 7. It is probably one of the most direct ways in which the divine partnership is revealed in Scripture. "Therefore humble yourselves under the mighty hand of God, that He may exalt you in due time, casting all your care upon Him, for He cares for you." We are not left to drift aimlessly through life. God has a divine purpose for our existence, and He will not leave us to wander aimlessly. Wherever you are right now, it is all in the purpose of God. God wants to equip you for the next level in the journey of life. If you don't expect God to lead, you will miss His direction.

God does not strip us of our dignity. When Peter was sinking and cried out, "Lord, save me!" (Matt. 14:30), Jesus saved him, and, rather than dragging Peter back to the boat all wet and dripping with water, they both walked back to the boat. We are elevated by virtue of our partnership with God. We see in the counsel of Peter the element of commitment—if we humble ourselves, God will exalt us in due time. When the going gets tough, don't quit! Your exaltation is nearer than when you first started!

Those who are humble are also people with integrity and commitment. Integrity says that we do not discount our God-given gifts and abilities but that we use them instead for their God-intended purpose. Humble people acknowledge their achievements and give credit to God. Humble people who accomplish great things do so because of the goodness of God. Moses was destined to be the instrument by which God would lead His people out of Egyptian bondage. Moses was off, however, on two fronts—on his timing and on his methods. Moses wanted to use his expertise and the time of his choosing without God's involvement. Consequently, he failed. When God was ready for Moses after forty years of deprogramming, Moses felt unfit and made a series of excuses, yet God overcame them all. God is not afraid to use people who, by all human standards, are unlikely candidates and consider themselves unlikely instruments. God has given you all that you need to fulfill His purpose. You are where you are for such a time as this.

Humility is something that we demonstrate in the way we live our lives. "Pride goes before destruction, and a haughty spirit before a fall" (Prov. 16:18). God consistently uses humble people. Even Jesus, who had every reason to be proud, humbled Himself and became obedient unto death, even death on the cross. His life was immersed in prayer and undergirded by an unwavering commitment to the values of heaven.

The fourth and final prerequisite for unhindered prayer is a willingness to learn. If we want to have unhindered prayer, we must be people of integrity, commitment, and humility, and we must have a willingness to learn. Jesus, the fountain of all wisdom, learned obedience by the things that He suffered (Heb. 5:8). "Jesus increased in wisdom and stature, and in favor with God and men" (Luke 2:52). Daniel learned the language and literature of the Babylonians. If our prayers are to be unhindered, we need to learn new ways of praying. We need to learn new things about the God to whom we pray. People who want to experience unhindered prayer need to be open to new ideas and to change. They need to not be afraid to learn. God's people will find that their prayer life will operate on high-octane when they pursue knowledge, humility, commitment, and integrity. Sin will no longer have dominion over them.

Unhindered prayer requires us to admit and confess our sins and to reorganize our behavior and attitudes so that they can fall in line with the divine ideal, as Ellen White points out:

> Prayer is not an expiation for sin; it has not virtue or merit of itself. All the flowery words at our command are not equivalent to one holy desire. The most eloquent prayers are but idle words if they do not express the true sentiments of the heart. But the prayer that comes from an earnest heart, when the simple wants of the soul are expressed, as we would ask an earthly friend for a favor, expecting it to be granted—this is the prayer of faith. God does not desire our ceremonial compliments, but the unspoken cry of the heart broken and subdued with a sense of its sin and utter weakness finds its way to the Father of all mercy." (*Prayer*, p. 60)

We can rest confidently in the fact that God wants to answer our prayer more than earthly fathers are willing to give good gifts to their children. God waits for us to come to Him in faith, knowing that He is at work always for our best good. We are to simply state our needs and claim His promises.

Begin today to set the stage for a future that is bright with answered prayers by being a person of integrity, commitment, and humility, with a willingness to learn all that is there to learn about a gracious heavenly Father.

## Chapter 6
# PRAYER AND SPIRITUALITY

Spirituality, while hard to measure, is certainly at the heart of who we are as Christians. It is the extent to which we resemble our Creator or the state of our being spiritual, that is, controlled by the Holy Spirit. Spirituality, however, does not happen by chance; we must be intentional about developing our spiritual side. So the question is: "How do we develop spirituality?" Peter provides us with a metaphor that I believe we can all identify with. As newborn infants need milk to grow and thrive, Christians need unadulterated spiritual milk so that we can grow by it in our salvation (1 Peter 2:2). Paul acknowledged the need to feed the believers in Corinth with milk because they were not able to take solid food (1 Cor. 3:2). The author of Hebrews pointed out that, because of spiritual immaturity, Christians, not understanding the principles of the Christian faith, had to be given milk (Heb. 5:12). Before his conversion, Paul (then called Saul) heard the voice from heaven saying, "Saul, Saul, why are you persecuting Me?" (Acts 9:4). Paul's response in verse 5 appears to be a prayer: "Who are You, Lord?" The context and God's directing him to Ananias in verse 11 strongly suggest that indeed it was a prayer.

Saul's circumstances forced him into the need for prayer. In fact, it was not just a momentary prayer like that of Peter when the waves separated him from Jesus. It was a payer that would be continuous. God said, "…go to the street called Straight, and inquire at the house of Judas for one called Saul of Tarsus, for behold, he is praying" (Acts 9:11). Prayer is a part of our devotional life, a spiritual discipline that connects us with the divine Spirit. It is the vehicle through which we come to God and acknowledge who we are and who He is. Prayer is the medium through which we send messages to God and receive messages from God. Since prayer is two-way communication, we must clear the channel so that information can flow freely. Prayer is choosing to allow the mind to dwell on the divine attributes, so that over time we can reflect those attributes in our lives. Prayer allows us to unplug from the material world and plug into the spiritual world through the process of the transformation of the mind. It is experiencing what Paul talks about in Romans 12:2—choosing not to conform to this world but to be transformed by the renewing of the mind.

> *Prayer is the medium through which we bare our hearts and souls before God*

Prayer is the medium through which we bare our hearts and souls before God. It is the spiritual discipline in which we allow ourselves to listen to what God has to say about Himself and about us. It is way we communicate our deepest fears and our highest joys. We can tell God what is on our minds, the mess that we are in, what is wrong with us, what is holding us back, who gets on our nerves, and who has broken our hearts or robbed us of our most prized possession.

A real devotional habit is developed over time as a result of a high degree of intentionality. It is during our time in prayer that we develop the art of unplugging from that which captures our attention in the earthly realm and, at the same time, plug into God and heavenly things. We must not think, however, that we can be or should be purely heavenly to the degree that we are misfits in this world. In fact, Jesus goes to the very heart of this matter in the Sermon on the Mount. He says we are to "seek first the kingdom of God and His righteousness, and all these things shall be added to us" (Matt. 6:31). What are these things? They are the things that the Gentiles seek first: what they eat, what they drink, and what they wear.

To plug into God requires intentional engagement, and it involves time alone with God, reading the Scriptures, and reflecting or meditating on Scripture, and connecting with God through the surrender of the will to His will. Plugging into God means being willing to ask Him what He wants me to do. I am sometimes so comfortable with what I am doing and where I am that I am not willing to ask that question. I want to continue in the old patterns and, as a result, communication is impeded.

Getting alone with God requires us to carve out a time and place in which distractions are reduced to a minimum. It is that special place where no one else can enter. For those who have the benefit of an office, that might be the place. For others, it might be the car on the way to or from work, or it might be some place out in nature. For still others, it might be a special room in the home. Wherever it is, it must be your special place, your holy and sacred place of divine-human encounter. When we emerge from our special place, it will also be said of us, as it was said of Peter and John, that men have taken notice that we have been with Jesus.

Getting alone with God means being in the very presence of God. Moses, after spending time in the presence of God, had to place a veil over his face because of the brightness of his countenance. When we spend time in God's presence, we can come out like Moses, with something special to offer to those around us, something more than our natural gifts or abilities, talents, ideas, or education.

Getting alone with God affords us rest from our human restlessness, rest from the taunts of Satan, rest from discomforting thoughts, rest from life's annoyances. It affords us entrance into a state of joy and peace. In it we acknowledge our sins and receive and appropriate God's forgiveness, unleashing the power of the Holy Spirit in our lives and enabling us to live a Spirit-filled life. Getting alone with God and being aware of His presence means an inner change. It is mind renewal, mind transformation. Paul highlights this transformation in words that indicate active engagement on our part. "Do not be conformed to this age, but be transformed by the renewing of your mind, so that you may discern what is that good, pleasing, and perfect will of God" (Rom. 12:2, HCSB).

Getting alone with God is opting to tap into everything He brings. God is infinite, which means that you will never be able to exhaust all that He offers of Himself. Nothing on earth compares to being plugged into God. Nothing. Once you have experienced it, everything on earth takes on new significance.

Getting alone with God allows us to come into an awareness of His sovereignty. God has His own reasons for responding to us in the manner that He does. He is essentially a God of love, and He is more interested in our knowing the Healer than in our experiencing the healing, more interested in our knowing the Deliverer than in our knowing deliverance, more interested in our knowing the Protector than in our having protection. It is all about the person and the relationship. "Faithful are the wounds of a friend, but the kisses of an enemy are deceitful" (Prov. 27:6).

Getting alone with God takes us beyond our preoccupation with behavior. It connects us with the power of heaven and changes the thoughts and feelings that drive behavior. It releases us from the burden of guilt and ushers us into health and wholeness. No longer do I have to perform to be accepted. I am accepted, therefore I perform. It is grace versus works. It is knowing that *"my sin, not in part but the whole is nailed to His cross and I bear it no more"* (Horatio Gates Spafford, "It Is Well With My Soul"). It leads me to the place where I find healing and form new habits. It is transformation.

We are to be mindful that the change takes place not merely because of the presence of God but in connection with our awareness of His presence. There has never been a time when God was not, and there has never been a place that God cannot be. God is from everlasting to everlasting, and He is omnipresent. God is fully present everywhere. David declared:

> Where can I go to escape Your Spirit? Where can I flee from Your presence? If I go up to heaven, You are there; if I make my bed in Sheol, You are there. If I live at the eastern horizon or settle at the western limits, even there Your hand will lead me; Your right hand will hold on to me. If I say, "Surely the darkness will hide me, and the light around me will be night"— even the darkness is not dark to You. The night shines like the day; darkness and light are alike to You. (Ps. 139:7–12, HCSB),

God is everywhere, and we can experience Him as the Alpha and Omega, the Beginning and the End. He knows everything about everyone and everything. Therefore, we cannot inform Him of anything, but all we can do is acknowledge in humility who we are in His presence.

Reading Scripture, as a part of one's prayer life, is more than reading for information; it is reading to develop a relationship—a relationship with Him who is the most awesome person in all the universe. He is the Friend who is closer than any relative. Scripture is God's divine self-disclosure. It is God painting a picture of Himself in the context of the divine-human relationship. It is through Scripture that we become aware of the presence of God. It is through Scripture that we know who we are because it describes our origin. Scripture tells us that God is Creator and that we are His creatures. Scripture tells us that we were created in the image of God. We rebelled against God, and God came in search of us, not as a vengeful God, but as a loving compassionate Redeemer.

Being aware of the presence of God makes all the difference in the way we live our lives. I am forever grateful to God for the nature of the relationship He had with David. David was not perfect. However, he, of all Bible characters, had one of the most fascinating relationships with God. David declared:

*Being aware of the presence of God makes all the difference in the way we live our lives*

> The lines have fallen to me in pleasant places; yes, I have a good inheritance. I will bless the LORD who has given me counsel; My heart also instructs me in the night seasons. I have set the LORD always before me; because He is at my right hand I shall not be moved. You will show me the path of life; in Your presence is fullness of joy; at Your right hand are pleasures forevermore. (Ps. 16:6–8, 11)

In the midst of life's conflicts, I can always step back and let God be God. I can have peace in the midst of life's storms. Why? Because

God is the Master of the universe. Nothing happens without His knowledge, and He is never taken by surprise. The presence of God is comforting because it suggests closeness. I am close to the very heart of God. Nothing can harm me when I am in His presence. In His presence is security, fullness of joy, sufficiency, abundant life, wholeness, and pleasures forevermore. In moments of confusion, I can find counsel in Him who is full of wisdom. In fact, He offers me wisdom liberally (James 1:5).

The reading of Scripture is not only for information but also for reflection and meditation. God counsels us to meditate on Scripture day and night because it is the foundation of right action, prosperity, and good success (Joshua 1:8). God did not simply make divine pronouncements, He chose a delivery system by which information can be delivered on a platform of relationship. Think about it—we are more prone to do things for the ones we love than for strangers. Why? Because of the relationship. Love empowers, transforms, enables, and controls us. Love works no ill to one's neighbor. Love fulfills God's law.

For years I have made it a habit to read the Bible through in the first quarter of the year, and it has always been a blessing. However, my greatest blessing has come when I have taken a verse or two of Scripture or a story about a particular person or event and have quietly reflected on it and asked, "What is it that God wants to say to me from this?" God never fails to speak, and that is the beauty of time spent with God in prayer.

We have seen that nearness to God brings lots of blessings in its train. Think about the significance of living in the shadow of the Almighty. David speaks, in Psalm 91, about the shadow of the Almighty as a secret place. That secret place suggests proximity, closeness. It is a location that no one else can go to except you. It is time alone with God. When we are there, nothing is impossible. "Impossible" is a fascinating word. It defines a circumstance or situation that is beyond human control. So, our finite limitations prepare us to receive the infinite. The impossibilities of earth prepare us for the possibilities of heaven. When life's darkest moments leave us impotent and all our efforts are exhausted, there is only one place to turn, and that is to heaven.

When God breaks through, all the glory and honor goes to Him. We cannot claim any of the victories. Think of the time that Peter was sinking beneath the waves on the storm-tossed Sea of Galilee. Jesus rescues us in our time of difficulty. He preserves our dignity, and we give Him all the glory.

It is reassuring to know that God waits to give us blessings that we would not otherwise receive if we did not ask. Yes, prayer allows us to communicate directly with God, our heavenly Father, who is more willing to give good gifts to us than earthly fathers are to give good gifts to their children. Think of the awesomeness of God and know that you are important to Him and that you have unimpeded access to Him every moment of every day.

## Chapter 7

# AUTHENTIC PRAYERS

Authenticity in prayer, whether private or public, is of utmost importance. While the Bible is filled with many examples of authentic prayer, I believe the premier example is modeled in the Lord's Prayer, which includes:

- Worship
- Submission
- Request
- Confession.

Jesus is the expert at praying. If we want to pray authentically, we should follow the principles that He gave. The well being of your prayer life determines the health of your spirituality. "God is Spirit, and those who worship Him must worship in spirit and truth" (John 4:24). So how can we develop an authentic prayer life? We do so as we do the following:

- Pray secretly
- Pray sincerely
- Pray specifically.

## Pray Secretly

In order to utilize these principles, we must get away from distractions by finding a secret place for prayer. David reminds us in Psalm 91:1, "He who dwells in the secret place of the Most High shall abide under the shadow of the Almighty." The Almighty provides refuge, protection, and deliverance.

A secret place does two things: It limits distractions, and it creates a special atmosphere. In our fast-paced world, with so many things screaming for our attention, we can be easily distracted. These distractions can come from anywhere—even religious sources. If you are a church worker, your emphasis on serving can sometimes squeeze out or bleed into your prayer time. Jesus understood this, and, as such, He would withdraw from the crowd to a mountain place to pray. At the most critical time in His life, just before Calvary, He took His disciples to the Garden of Gethsemane. He left eight disciples in one area and took Peter, James, and John a little further where He left them as He went a little further Himself to pray. Jesus physically removed Himself from the distraction. We too must be intentional in removing ourselves from things or people that would distract us during our time of prayer.

Closely associated with distraction is atmosphere. The creation of a proper atmosphere is very important. How do we do this? By reducing noise from whatever source, by clearing the clutter, unfinished work, or anything else that could cause our minds to wander off. One way to remove a distraction is to make it a part of the prayer. For example, if your thoughts begin to be drawn away by some unfinished business, you might want to say something such as, "Lord, even now as I'm seeking you, my mind is being overwhelmed by thoughts of other things. I surrender these things into Your capable hands and ask that You would reveal Your purpose for me at this very moment."

It is important to stay in the moment and allow God to be present in the moment as well. What was at first a distraction has become a pathway to a new dimension of your prayer and an opportunity for you to see God at work in that moment. Distractions, when once recognized, can become a prayer-enhancing tool to make

> *Distractions, when once recognized, can become a prayer-enhancing tool to make your prayer life stronger and more meaningful*

your prayer life stronger and more meaningful. While we want the very best atmosphere for our prayer time, we cannot afford to allow the lack of the best atmosphere to stop us from praying. It is here that we see the value of Paul's counsel to pray without ceasing. Pray whether you think the atmosphere is right or not. Invite the God of the universe to create order in the midst of your confusion.

## Pray Sincerely

To pray sincerely is to avoid the use of vain babbling or meaningless phrases. Don't ask God to do what he has already said He will do. For example, we should not ask God to be with us when He has said, "... lo, I am with you always, even to the end of the age" (Matt. 28:20). "Let your conduct be without covetousness; be content with such things as you have. For He Himself has said, 'I will never leave you nor forsake you'" (Heb. 13:5).

He is also "Immanuel, . . . God with us" (Matt. 1:23). As long as He is God, He is with us. What we should ask for is that God would enable us to be aware of His presence. When we think we need to ask Him to be with us, we are actually saying that God waits to be directed by us. He is no longer autonomous, and He really doesn't care to be around us. God is omnipresent and omniscient. More importantly, He is our loving, heavenly Father—not an absentee landlord.

We should remember that we are talking to a loving Father, and we should talk to Him authentically, reverently, personally, and earnestly. God is not interested in pet phrases. Psalm 62:8 declares, "Pour out your heart before Him." Tell Him how you feel today and what you are thinking. He can handle anything you can throw at Him. In fact, God is always ahead of the curve. He knows your thoughts before you are aware of them yourself. He says, "Casting all your care upon Him, for He cares for you" (1 Peter 5:7).

Praying specifically, then, means that we name what we need from God and we keep a record of His response. If you need forgiveness for a particular sin such as lying to your friend during the day, resist the temptation to say, "Lord, forgive me of all my sins." Rather, name the sin and the circumstances surrounding it so that you can break the power of that sin over your life. Being sincere means being specific. It adds authenticity to your prayers.

## Pray Specifically

Focus on God's ability—not on your worth. God already loves you more than you can ever imagine. "...before they call, I will answer; and while they are still speaking, I will hear" (Isa. 65:24). I am always impressed with friends who are so in tune with me that they anticipate my needs and respond just at the right moment. God, my heavenly Father, is not only capable of responding to my needs at the right time, but He knows everything that I need and has put in place the resource to meet all my needs. The Lord's Prayer is a great example of how to pray specifically.

*First, submit your will to God's will. Let God's will be first in your*

- Marriage
- Finances
- Family
- Care of your body
- Career
- Relationships
- Ministry
- Business.

You can be sure that the One who made you knows more about you and has a vested interest in your optimum performance and well being. He has a purpose for you that is beyond anything you could ever imagine.

*Second, God is interested in your nutrition.* "Give us this day our daily bread" (Matt. 6:11). From the very beginning, God outlined what the very best diet plan would be for us so that we can perform at optimum level. During the ministry of Jesus, He took time to feed the hungry, in keeping with the test of the true fast—to "deal thy bread to the hungry" (Isa. 58:7, KJV). He reminded us not to worry about what we should eat or drink. We know experientially that what we are going to eat can be a constant source of anxiety. Yet, we can lay all our concerns before Him. "Be anxious for nothing, but in everything by prayer and supplication, with thanksgiving, let your requests be made known to God; and the peace of God, which surpasses all understanding, will guard your hearts and minds through Christ Jesus" (Phil. 4:6, 7).

God directed Adam and Eve to eat from specific trees in the garden (Gen. 1:29). And Paul teaches us, "Whether you eat or drink, or whatever you do, do all to the glory of God" (1 Cor. 10:31).

***Third, we must be sure that we are not the problem.*** We are to live with a forgiving spirit towards others. Forgiveness—we are sometimes confused about it. We think that forgiving is forgetting. However, forgiveness is, first, a gift to ourselves and, second, a process that takes place over time. Until I am willing to accept the hurt that has been inflicted on me, I will not be in a frame of mind in which I can forgive. I think about it like this: If I want to be forgiven, I need to forgive those who have offended me. Jesus offered objective forgiveness when, on the cross, He declared, "Father, forgive them, for they do not know what they do" (Luke 23:34). We, too, must be in a state of readiness to do the same. "Forgive us our debts, as we forgive our debtors" (Matt. 6:12).

***Fourth, end your prayer with more worship.*** "For Yours is the kingdom and the power and the glory forever" (Matt. 6:13). We pray authentically by following this pattern:

- Worship—focusing on God's attributes
- Submission—surrendering our will to His
- Request—God wants us to ask based on His purpose, not ours
- Confession—We must be specific, saying, for example, "Lord, I have been unkind to my neighbor." "I have cheated on my exam today."

We can subconsciously get to the place that we think the power and the glory really belong to us—that is, until we are confronted with the impossible. Authentic prayer is not a time for us to boast; it is a time for God to shine in our lives. To Him be the power and the glory!

## How to start praying specifically

Write out your prayers and then read them to God. It forces you to concentrate. At the end of a week or a month, re-read your prayers and make note of the ones that God has answered. If writing is not your thing, find a method that is. By all means make your prayers private, sincere, and specific. It is the Jesus model. Remember that God's supernatural power is released through prayer.

God is interested in you and your needs. He can meet any need and has invited you to come to Him with all your needs. He is not far, far away; He is near. He is here. He is always with you. He is the powerful Creator of the world, and He created it for you. For God to begin releasing His supernatural power in your life, you must begin to pray. Why not begin right now? Your loving heavenly Father is waiting.

## Chapter 8

# LESSONS FOR FATHERS FROM A MODEL PRAYER

> *"In this manner, therefore, pray:*
> *Our Father in heaven,*
> *Hallowed be Your name.*
> *Your kingdom come.*
> *Your will be done*
> *On earth as it is in heaven.*
> *Give us this day our daily bread.*
> *And forgive us our debts,*
> *As we forgive our debtors,*
> *And do not lead us into temptation,*
> *But deliver us from the evil one.*
> *For Yours is the kingdom and the power and the glory forever.*
> *Amen." (Matt. 6:9–13)*

Jesus gave this prayer to His disciples in response to the request they made after observing His prayer life. While the wording quoted above comes from Matthew's rendering of the prayer, it was Luke who indicated that Jesus gave it in response to the disciples' request, "Lord, teach us to pray, as John also taught his disciples" (Luke 11:1). So the question is: What can fathers learn from this prayer to make their own prayer life authentic and exemplary? If a father's prayer can be hindered by the way he treats his wife, certainly he can learn something from the very best Father in the universe, as we pointed out in Chapter 5.

This prayer is not only instructive, but it reflects a deeply spiritual set of values—a set of values that will set us apart from the rest of the people around us who do not subscribe to those values. This prayer challenges us to rise to new heights in our role as fathers and to slay the dragon of complacency. So here we go. Let's look at the prayer to learn meaningful lessons.

## Fathers are to be on location (v. 9)

One of the key characteristics of our heavenly Father is that He is omnipresent, which means that He is present everywhere. While earthly fathers cannot be present everywhere, they should be present in the life of their children—emotionally, physically, socially, mentally, and spiritually. There is no good substitute for a father. In our society today, too many fathers are absent, and their absence has caused untold harm. We have too many children who suffer on multiple levels because their fathers are absent. Boys grow up not knowing what it's like to be a man and a father; girls grow up not knowing and enjoying the model they should have for relating to males or their future husband. God said of Abraham, "I know him, that he will command his children and his household after him" (Gen. 18:19, KJV). For Abraham to fulfill that godly declaration, he had to be present. Fathers, can you identify with your children's needs if you are not present? Can you provide the emotional, physical, social, and spiritual needs of your children if you are not present? Our heavenly Father encourages us to call on Him at any time, especially when we are in trouble. But lest you think you only need to call on Him in times of trouble, He reminds us that "before we call, He will answer; and while we are still speaking, He will hear" (Isa. 65:24, paraphrase). He further declares, "I will never leave you nor forsake you" (Heb. 13:5). That is awesome stuff! That is commitment! God our heavenly Father is committed to being there for the long haul. Talk of being ready and available! Fathers, our children should know that we will always be there for them—ready and available in good times and in bad, committed to them and their well-being regardless of the circumstances.

Our heavenly Father teaches us that, in order to meet the needs of our children, we must be present. We must be present for their parent-teacher conferences and their extracurricular events, for family worship, for vacations, and for the changing periods of our children's maturation. Fathers, you are to be there—lovingly, supportively, always looking out for what is best for your children.

## Fathers are to earn the respect of others (v. 9)

While Scripture says that children are to honor their parents that their days may be long upon the land (Eph. 6:3), how can children honor and show respect to someone who is not present? To earn something, one must work, *demonstrating* that they are worthy of their respect. Respect suggests proximity, being within range. Fathers, make it easy for your children to fulfill the command to honor you by being present—present physically, emotionally, socially, and spiritually.

> *Our heavenly Father teaches us that, in order to meet the needs of our children, we must be present*

When it comes to spiritual direction, it's the father's fundamental right and responsibility to lead. Joshua, at a critical time in Israel's history, much like ours today, was not afraid to stand up and say, "But as for me and my house, we will serve the LORD" (Joshua 24:15). This declaration was made in response to Israel's widespread departure from their God-given spiritual moorings. Somehow it was more pleasing to be like everyone else. Fathering is not a popularity contest. It is a sacred duty that cannot be ignored without serious consequences. The eternal destiny of our children rests on how well we do our jobs. It is not uncommon to hear fathers say, "I don't know what is happening to my child." Some fathers say, "I don't force my child to give his or her life to Christ." Yet, at the same time, that father would not let that child *not* go to school simply because the child didn't feel like it. Fathers, your children might not like your stance on spiritual things. However, if you are consistent in your spiritual walk and you set a godly example, then you will earn your child's respect.

Fathers, when your child reaches a certain level of maturity, and they decide to go another way, that is their choice. Respect it, and they will still respect you for your consistency. Our heavenly Father gives us the power of choice, and He allows us to exercise that choice. He does not force us to do anything. We are all free moral agents, and we are responsible for the choices that we make.

## Fathers should have a domain and possession over which they have control (v. 10)

Fathers are to remember the wise words of Solomon, "A good man leaves an inheritance to his children's children, but the wealth of the sinner is stored up for the righteous" (Prov. 13:22). Fathers are to be good managers of their resources; they are to exercise good judgment in the management of that which has been entrusted to them. Fathers are to save for the future. They are to be future oriented—not only in the management of their resources but also in the training of their offspring—so that the principal will be maintained and compounded with interest.

In Luke 15:11, 12, Jesus illustrates this lesson by showing how fathers are expected to have something to pass on to the next generation. He begins: "A certain man had two sons. And the younger of them said to his father. 'Father, give me the portion of goods that falls to me.' So he divided to them his livelihood." Our heavenly Father sets the tone by freely giving to us. In Genesis 1:29, God said, "See I have given you every herb that yields seed which is on the face of the earth, and every tree whose fruit yields seed; to you it shall be for food." Mankind had free access to all of God's creation, and we were to be stewards of that creation. We were to have dominion over it. Through stewardship of the earth, God taught the first humans lessons of responsibility. Good stewardship of God's creation would ensure continued sufficiency. Their needs would always be met.

Fathers are the head of their homes and their estates. They are called *house-bands* because they hold the house and home together. They are the heads of their homes and, as such, they are to have dominion over it, to dispense it as they see fit. Fathers are instructed not to frustrate their children but to bring them up in the fear and admonition of the Lord (Eph. 6:4). So, when the younger son, in the story, came and asked for the portion of goods that fell to him, the father gave it without hesitation. But then the son wasted it and suffered the consequences. His eventual deprivation led him not only to think of his father's house but also to return to it with a humble acknowledgment that he had sinned and had no more right to his father's estate.

Our heavenly Father sets the tone for fathers. The earth belongs to Him. However, He does not rule with an iron hand. Not only does the earth belong to Him, but we also are His. We are so valuable to Him that He was willing to send His Son to give His very life for us, and the Father suffered with the Son as He hang upon the cross. Yet, God does not use force. Though He has the power to compel as He wants, He refuses to use that power. Rather, He pleads with us on the basis of love to acknowledge His will. Fathers, what an example to follow is this. We are to be willing to pour out our very lives for our children and to do it in such a way that they never ever question the genuineness of our love and commitment to them. Pour out your life for them even when they (as well as you) know that they are not deserving of it. Love is the greatest force in the world. As Paul writes: Love "bears all things, believes all things, hopes all things, endures all things" (1 Cor. 13:7).

## Fathers are to be makers of rules that are fair, clear, and reasonable (v. 10)

Fathers, or husbands, are called upon to "love your wives, just as Christ also loved the church and gave Himself for her, that He might sanctify and cleanse her with the washing of water by the word, that He might present her to Himself a glorious church, not having spot or wrinkle or any such thing, but that she should be holy and without blemish" (Eph. 5:25–27).

When rules that are made for the good of others are based on love, those rules will never become an end in themselves. They will be reasonable and will never be enforced recklessly but only thoughtfully and lovingly. The benefits of those rules to others will be clearly seen, and, when those rules are broken, the consequences should not simply be punishment but a clear disadvantage in the quality of life for the rule breaker. Rules are beneficial to all. They provide consistency, guide behavior, and ensure safety and security. Fathers, therefore, are to pray and seek God's wisdom in establishing rules that are fair, clear, and reasonable and that will enable the family to fulfill its divine purpose.

> *When rules that are made for the good of others are based on love, those rules will never become an end in themselves*

## Fathers are providers (v. 11)

First Timothy 5:8 makes it clear that, if a man does "not provide for his own, and especially for those of his household, he has denied the faith and is worse than an unbeliever."

Jesus instructed His disciples to ask for their daily bread, not because their heavenly Father would not give it to them were they not to ask but because it would remind them of their dependence on the Father and His ability and willingness to provide their needs. Fathers are to be the breadwinners of their home. Children should never have to worry about what they are going to eat. It is a sad state of affairs when children have to provide for themselves or depend on strangers. According to Paul, it is a denial of faith not to provide for one's family.

Our heavenly Father maintains a daily connection with His children by being present to give them sustenance on a daily basis. For forty years, God guided, protected, and provided for Israel in the wilderness. He also miraculously preserved the food prepared on the sixth day for the seventh day of the week when food left over during the other six weekly days would spoil. Genesis also lets us know that God made provision for our daily bread. Fathers, if you are not prepared to provide for your children, then maybe you should think twice before fathering children. Our heavenly Father set us an example by making everything we would ever need *before* making us.

## Fathers are to be sensitive to the weaknesses of their families and are to be willing to forgive (v. 12)

This portion of the model prayer demonstrates to fathers that they don't have to be total paragons of virtue to be a good father. It teaches us to see ourselves as fallible human beings who can be comfortable with our own vulnerability. Consequently, we also need forgiveness. We must forgive as we are forgiven. When we discover that we have offended our children or have been negligent in the execution of our duties, we must willingly ask forgiveness. In fact, it is a great way to model forgiveness for our children and endear ourselves to them. Fathers can use their moments of vulnerability to show their children how to show empathy.

In Luke 15, we have a wonderful example of how to show empathy—listen carefully, make suggestions tentatively, be an encourager, and wait patiently for the opportunity to share Christ's love. On the cross, Jesus offered objective forgiveness in the words, "Father, forgive them, for they do not know what they do" (Luke 23:34). Through this act, Jesus was making it clear that forgiveness is available to whoever it is that needs it, and He was setting the example that we too must be willing and ready to forgive.

> And the son said to him, "Father I have sinned against heaven and in your sight, and am no longer worthy to be called your son." But the father said to his servants, "Bring out the best robe and put it on him, and put a ring on his hand and sandals on his feet. And bring the fatted calf here and kill it, and let us eat and be merry; for this my son was dead and is alive again; he was lost and is found." And they began to be merry. (Luke 15:21–24)

In verses 31 and 32, the father addresses the older son in what I would consider one of the clearest examples of empathy in

Scripture. The older brother begins his angry remarks, "As soon as this son of yours" (v. 30), not "As soon as my brother ..." The father responds by referring to the older brother as "son," maintaining their connection. "And he said to him, 'Son, you are always with me, and all that I have is yours. It was right that we should make merry and be glad, for your brother was dead and is alive again, and was lost and is found" (v. 32).

Fathers, there will be times when you will be tempted to remind your children of how they have wasted that which you have worked so hard to obtain and to join their siblings in disowning them, but—I plead with you—resist the temptation, and use the opportunity to wisely model empathy. Listen carefully; make suggestions tentatively. Be an encourager, and wait for an opportunity to share Christ. Take the path less traveled. You will be glad you did. That is what our heavenly Father modeled for us in the beginning when man sinned. He was fully aware of the precise moment that Adam sinned. Yet, He did not rush into the garden in panic mode with a "How could you?" attitude. Rather, He came at their usual time of meeting and gently called, "Adam, where are you?" Can you hear the entreaty in the father's voice in Jesus' parable? "Son, you are always with me, and all that I have is yours. It was right that we should make merry and be glad, for your brother was dead and is alive again, and was lost and is found" (v. 32).

Fathers, when you are tempted to panic and rush headlong into a situation, take some time to reflect and ask yourself the question, "How can I use this opportunity to show Christ's love to the erring one?" Don't miss an opportunity to share Christ, and, should you miss the opportunity, be quick to confess and to ask for forgiveness.

## Fathers are to be protectors of the family on multiple levels—emotionally, physically, mentally, and, most importantly, spiritually (v. 13)

"And you, fathers, do not provoke your children to wrath, but bring them up in the training and admonition of the Lord" (Eph. 6:4).

"Train up a child in the way he should go, and when he is old he will not depart from it" (Prov. 22:6).

"And these words which I command you today shall be in your heart. You shall teach them diligently to your children, and shall talk of them when you sit in your house, when you walk by the way, when you lie down, and when you rise up. You shall bind them as a sign on your hand, and they shall be as frontlets between your eyes. You shall write them on the doorposts of your house and on your gates" (Deut. 6:6–9).

It is clear that the Word of God is the surest source of protection for our children. They are to be saturated with the Word. Fathers are to take every opportunity to teach their children the Word of God. David wrote, "Your word I have hidden in my heart, that I might not sin against You" (Ps. 119:11). The Word protects on multiple levels. It brings to the obedient a sense of peace. It guides. It makes us wise. It fortifies.

## A father is to be acknowledged and affirmed by those of his household (v. 13)

Wives, here is where you can be instrumental in affirming fatherhood. You do so by being the kind of wife that allows your husband to safely trust you. Be lavish but sincere in your praise for your husband in the presence of your children. Affirm his efforts to be the provider and protector of his family. When he takes steps to plan for the future, let him know that you value and appreciate every effort he makes. How you respond to your husband will be instructive for your children.

Fathers, when you have done your best in being the father that God intended you to be, then kingdom power and glory belongs to you. As long as you function in God's intended role for you, kingdom power and glory will always be yours. Your children will rise up and call you blessed. Yours will be the reward of seeing your children grow up as trees of righteousness. As a father, don't just pray the Lord's Prayer mindlessly; learn how to be the very best father you can be. You will be glad you did.

## CHAPTER 9

# DON'T BE ANXIOUS! JUST PRAY

There are many things that can cause us to be anxious today, such as the illness of a family member, a friend, a colleague, or someone with whom we are in a special relationship. Anxiety can be caused by a variety of factors, effecting our financial, physical, spiritual, emotional, and mental health. However, the One who made us says we are not to be anxious. Look at the way the Apostle Paul shares this vital information in Philippians 4:6, 7, writing, by the way, while confined in prison.

> "Be anxious for nothing, but in everything by prayer and supplication, with thanksgiving, let your requests be made known to God; and the peace of God, which surpasses all understanding, will guard your hearts and minds through Christ Jesus" (Phil. 4:6, 7).

The force of this command rests on the veracity of the One who gave it. He is our Creator, Redeemer, and Friend. He is almighty and omnipresent. Of all our friends, He is the most reliable; He is the One who will never leave us or forsake us. So, when He says, "Don't be anxious," He means it. He really doesn't want us to worry about anything, regardless of what it might be. Jesus, in His maiden sermon, otherwise known as the Sermon on the Mount, went to great lengths to let us know that we don't need to be anxious. I believe the length of this passage conveys the depth of His concern for us and how important it is for us to get the message—especially in our day when there is so much that we are not sure about.

> Therefore I say to you, do not worry about your life, what you will eat or what you will drink; nor about your body, what you will put on. Is not life more than food and the body more than clothing? Look at the birds of the air, for they neither sow nor reap nor gather into barns; yet your heavenly Father feeds them. Are you not of more value than they? Which of you by worrying can add one cubit to his stature? So why do you worry about clothing? Consider the lilies of the field, how they grow: they neither toil nor spin; and yet I say to you that even Solomon in all his glory was not arrayed like one of these. Now if God so clothes the grass of the field, which today is, and tomorrow is thrown into the oven, will He not much more clothe you, O you of little faith? Therefore do not worry, saying, "What shall we eat?" or "What shall we drink?" or "What shall we wear?" For after all these things the Gentiles seek. For your heavenly Father knows that you need all these things. But seek first the kingdom of God and His righteousness, and all these things shall be added to you. Therefore do not worry about tomorrow, for tomorrow will worry about its own things. Sufficient for the day is its own trouble." (Matt. 6:25–34)

Six times in the passage Jesus used the phrase "don't worry," or a variation of it. Could it be that He is asking, "When are you going to get it through your thick head that you do not need to worry?"

Those who pursue food and clothing while neglecting God and His will for their lives are choosing to go the difficult way. God, who owns everything and is madly in love with us, says, "I want to give it all to you, and you are still going after it the wrong way." He says, "Ask of Me, and I will give You the nations for Your inheritance, and the ends of the earth for Your possession" (Ps. 2:8). Or, as He personally addressed the issue of fear that the disciples were facing in Luke 12:32, He empathically declared, "Do not fear, little flock, for it is your Father's good pleasure to give you the kingdom."

God wants to give us more than just the nations. He wants to give us the entire kingdom. We serve an unlimited God. He is a God of sufficiency. The meeting of needs is a part of the divine DNA. It is a principle of God's kingdom. It is buried in the principle of sowing and reaping.

But this I say: He who sows sparingly will also reap sparingly, and he who sows bountifully will also reap bountifully. So let each one give as he purposes in his heart, not grudgingly or of necessity; for God loves a cheerful giver. And God is able to make all grace abound toward you, that you, always having all sufficiency in all things, may have an abundance for every good work. (2 Cor. 9:6–8)

## Don't worry. Just pray

The disciples—as well as the vast multitude—were doubtlessly worrying about dealing with the demands of life. But, Jesus saw what they could not. He saw what they had while they were concerned with what they did not have. When we constantly look at the failures of the past and the uncertainties of the future, we cannot see the possibilities or the joys of the present. You already have everything that you need to meet all your needs. When we take what we have and mingle it with faith and obedience, it will inevitably be more than enough. Failure to do so results in anxiety and worry, and then worry takes over as the order of the day. Worry grows when we think about a problem over and over without seeing a solution.

> *When we constantly look at the failures of the past and the uncertainties of the future, we cannot see the possibilities or the joys of the present*

The phrase, "Your heavenly Father knows that you need all these things," is important. It is God's way of reminding us of His capacity to meet our present and future needs.

Today, as we face the challenges that will surely come our way, let us purpose in our hearts that we will not be intimidated by them but that we will focus, rather, on our all-sufficient God and experience His peace. He is able to do much more than we are able to ask or think.

Think of what this means. No matter how idealistic our thoughts and requests, God can exceed them into infinity. Let us take the message of Helen H. Lemmel seriously.

> O soul, are you weary and troubled?
> No light in the darkness you see?
> There's light for a look at the Savior,
> And life more abundant and free!
> Turn your eyes upon Jesus,
> Look full in His wonderful face;
> And the things of this world will grow strangely dim
> In the light of His glory and grace.

Your need pales into insignificance in the presence of an all-powerful God. His ability to provide is unparalleled. He who stepped out into space and spoke and it was done, commanded and it stood fast, is just as powerful today.

The uncertainty of our times should drive us to the Savior rather than to worry. The mighty angels of God are still "holding the four winds of the earth, that the winds should not blow on the earth, on the sea, or on any tree" (Rev. 7:1). We can trust the great God of the universe to keep His promise. It is the certainty of that promise that should release us from anxiety. God's grace is a sure anchor for the praying, trusting child of God. The ministry of the Holy Spirit is readily available. Let the leaders of the nations act with seeming disregard for the teaching of Scripture. They will soon be stripped of their power because God's Word will not fail, when it says: "The kingdoms of this world have become the kingdoms of our Lord and of His Christ, and He shall reign forever and ever" (Rev. 11:15).

Be anxious for nothing. Just pray. You are God's child. As a child, you have a right; you have access; you have a past, a present, and a future. Your past failures are blotted out; your present challenges are being met with the all-sufficiency of your Father in heaven; and your future is certain and secure.

## Chapter 10

# PRAYER IN EVERYTHING

"Be anxious for nothing, but in everything by prayer and supplication, with thanksgiving, let your requests be made known to God; and the peace of God, which surpasses all understanding, will guard your hearts and minds through Christ Jesus" (Phil. 4:6, 7). To the modern mind, it seems almost impossible not to be anxious while praying in everything. In fact, even among Christians, there are those who do not believe that we should pray in everything or that such prayer is even possible. Yet, if we are to enjoy the benefits that God offers, we must communicate with Him at all times in everything and about everything.

What God offers is peace from on high, wrapped up in His Son, Jesus Christ. When we read John 3:16, "For God so loved the world that He gave His only begotten Son, that whoever believes in Him should not perish but have everlasting life," we are reflecting on the ultimate gift of Heaven. God's gift comes with everything that we could possibly need to live life without anxiety. Paul reinforces the fact that Jesus is our peace, in writing: "For He Himself is our peace …" The wall of separation is broken down, and we are reconciled to God (Eph. 2:14, 15). Through Jesus, we have access to the Father by the Spirit.

The force of the phrase, "Be anxious for nothing but in every thing with prayer and supplication," is amazing. We are invited to communicate with the Creator God, the Alpha and Omega, the omniscient, omnipresent God, the One who controls the universe.

Knowing that He is sovereign over everything that concerns us means that we can pray about our cares, concerns, and trials, our struggles and joys, our finances, family relationships, homes and cars, our hopes and dreams and vacations. We can pray about things that are lost, about our hurts, failures, and victories, about our work and our worship. And on and on the list goes. Nothing is too big or too small to talk about to God.

God wants us to know that it is better to pray than to be anxious because, when we pray, He unleashes His power in our lives and transforms either our outlook or our circumstances. More often than not, it is we who experience the change. We are drawn to see the circumstances from a different perspective. With the unleashing of God's power comes peace and contentment. The fact that God's peace comes in a neatly packaged Person—in Jesus—should give us cause to trust Him more.

The experience of Jesus with His disciples on the storm tossed Sea of Galilee, recorded in Mark 4:35–41, reminds me of the depth of this peace. While Jesus was peacefully sleeping within the boat, the disciples were frantically bailing out water, trying to save themselves from going under. As they realized that their efforts were no match for the storm, they turned accusingly to Jesus and exclaimed, "Teacher, do You not care that we are perishing!" Like the disciples, we sometimes forget that Jesus is in the midst of the situation with us. We sometimes think that we know more than Jesus or that Jesus really does not care about what we are going through. However, this story teaches us that, even in the most threatening of life's circumstances, Jesus is present. We simply need to refocus our attention on Him, the Problem-solver. Jesus did not allow Himself to be drawn away to chase the proverbial rabbit. Rather, He spoke to the wind, and the wind obeyed Him. Jesus then turned to the disciples, who were now filled with amazement, and asked, "How is it that you have no faith?"

Jesus' question called their attention to introspection, while they had looked for someone to blame. What do you do when you are in over your head? Do you look for someone or something to blame, or do you seek to draw on your inner reserve? God made you with all the resources you need to deal with anything that

He allows to come your way. The challenges are custom made to draw out that which He has placed within you. They are all pre-approved, instruments designed to fulfill His purpose. You might not feel like it or understand it, but God gives only good gifts, and what might appear to be for evil is intended for good. Stop and take a second look. Remember what Joseph said to his brothers—years after they sold him as a slave: "You meant it for evil, but God meant it for good to save many lives" (Gen. 50:20, paraphrase).

The day of the storm on the lake, the disciples were not only able to see the power of Jesus in a new and fresh way, but they were also able to recognize their need to grow in a trusting relationship with their Teacher.

Have you ever felt as though a problem was about to destroy you—a problem that was so big that no amount of effort on your part would make a difference? A careful perusal of the Scriptures will reveal that there are several Bible characters who felt the same way before they cried out to God.

God loves to walk calmly into our chaos. He enjoys taking on our impossible situations because, ultimately, He will shine. He gets the glory, and we are drawn more to Him. Our recognition of His presence changes everything. When He comes into view, our circumstances are transformed, our storms are calmed, and our hopelessness becomes hopeful. We can now focus on living rather than on perishing.

No longer were the disciples thinking about survival. They were exclaiming, "Who can this be, that even the wind and the sea obey Him!" (Mark 4:41). Could it be that God allows the problem you are facing right now so that you can see Him in a new and fresh light? Could it be that, in your weakness, God wants you to see His strength? Could it be that, in your ignorance, He wants you to see His wisdom? Truthfully, James declares, "If any of you lacks wisdom, let him as of God, who gives to all liberally and without reproach, and it will be given to him" (James 1:5).

Yes, God will give each of us what we need. His capability is beyond human comprehension. In the beginning, He stepped out into space and spoke, and the material world came into existence. Our God is the Creator. Therefore, when He says that we are to pray in everything, He is not offering empty words. The creative power of the universe is behind them. God is eternally powerful and forever faithful. Our circumstances may seek to draw us down, but God's love seeks to lift us up. So, don't be afraid. Go ahead and take Paul's counsel seriously. "In everything by prayer and supplication, with thanksgiving, let your requests be made known" (Phil. 4:6).

We are all potentially wealthy because Jesus, who was rich, became poor so that we, through His poverty, might become rich. Jesus took our nothingness and gave us His "some-thing-ness." We can hold onto our nothingness, or we can let go of it and take hold of that which Jesus gives so lovingly and freely.

## Why should we pray in everything?

We should pray in everything because, when we are at our worst, God is at His best. He draws close through the power of His grace to heal the brokenness of our blame-based society. Yes, God's grace is greater than all our sins. Our sins have all been nailed to His cross, and we bear them no more. They are cast into the depths of the sea, and God will remember them no more. Peter blamed Jesus, but Jesus challenged him to look at what He had already given him—faith. Is there something that God has already given you that you are not using while you are trying to blame God?

*We should pray in everything because, when we are at our worst, God is at His best*

When we learn the art of praying in everything, we will replace injustice with justice and privilege; we will replace racism with rights, harassment with respect and honor, fear with faith, rejection with acceptance, and hate with love. In everything, no matter how painful it may be, we will commit our inner world to God. Yes, we will be characterized by an inner peace that the world cannot take away.

When we pray in everything, we will become fruitful in the land of our affliction. Our wilderness will not be a place that we long to get out of but, rather, a place where we hear God's voice and find our own. As it was with John the Baptist, so it will be with us—living in the wilderness will be a badge of honor. We will learn the true meaning of Romans 8:28, "And we know that all things work together for good to those who love God, to those who are the called according to His purpose." Yes, God has a purpose buried in your pain. God's purpose is beautiful, refreshing, invigorating, and transforming. Very often it is only in the land of pain that love, joy, peace, patience, gentleness, goodness, meekness, temperance, and faith are produced. It is just that radical. Tragedy gives way to triumph, the impossible to the possible, the ordinary to the extraordinary, and the unbelievable to the believable.

When we pray in everything, we are drawn to see God's purpose. We "are all sons of God through faith in Christ Jesus" (Gal. 3:26). God's original purpose is that we would be like Him. We were made in His image. Consequently, we can choose to be like Him, or we can continue in our rebellion.

When the circumstances of life turn against you and the evil of the world slams you to the ground, will it break your spirit and make you let go of God? Or will those very circumstances change you and give you power, prosperity, and prestige? Will you give them to God? Will you use them for His glory? There are times when God uses either pain or pleasure to test you. Sometimes pleasure is a greater test than pain. Solomon had a hard time with pleasure. In fact, he flunked that test and finally concluded, "There is a way that seems right to a man, but its end is the way of death" (Prov. 16:25). Paul, on the other hand, handled pain with courage, as we find reflected in 2 Corinthians 4:8–11, 15:

> We are hard-pressed on every side, yet not crushed; we are perplexed, but not in despair; persecuted, but not forsaken; struck down, but not destroyed—always carrying about in the body the dying of the Lord Jesus, that the life of Jesus also may be manifested in our body... For all things are for your sakes, that grace, having spread through the many, may cause thanksgiving to abound to the glory of God.

When we pray in everything, we will receive God's boundless blessings; our faith will increase; God will give us new revelations and patience to wait on Him. We will not be moved by the pit or the palace because the issue is not the "what" but the "who." God "is able to do exceedingly abundantly above all that we ask or think" (Eph. 3:20). He will reveal to us great and mighty things, which we do not now know. He will cause those who wait on Him to "mount up with wings like eagles," to "run and not be weary," and to "walk and not faint" (Isa. 40:31).

## Chapter 11

# LISTEN—GOD IS SPEAKING

"Be still, and know that I am God" (Ps. 46:10). When we pray, we tend to think that it is our role to speak and God's role to listen. However, if we approach prayer as conversation, then listening becomes an important part of the exchange. In communication, the speaker delivers a message and the listener receives a message. However, in order for communication to be meaningful, the message sent must be the message received. The speaker must make a conscious effort to communicate the message as simply as possible, and the listener must clear his or her mind of any distractions so the message can be received. In other words, for effective communication to take place, there must be a meeting of the minds regarding the purpose of the exchange.

When God says, "Be still, and know that I am God" (Ps. 46:10), the context suggests that God was sending Israel a message, but Israel was not listening. God was saying to Israel, I am your protector and defender. Yet, the people of Israel were attempting to protect and defend themselves. Hence, God said, "Stop doing what you are doing, and hear what I am saying by what I am doing."

Think about the times that you have been in difficult circumstances and have tried desperately to handle the situation on your own. Yet, then, in utter desperation, you turned to God. God was always there, though perhaps standing in the shadows.

The God who knows everything and can do anything, who is everywhere present, and who loves you without measure, waits patiently to help.

Direct communication is determined by the speaker's intent. What is it that you want from or want to see in your hearer? Is it a change of behavior? Is it reassurance or support, companionship, or clarification on a particular position or issue? Failing to state your purpose means risking confusion. Simply telling God what we want and giving Him thanks for what He has already done makes Him less than the God He is. God speaks to us through Scripture, through human relationships, and through the Holy Spirit, nature, and life's circumstances. If we are going to hear God, we must be intentional. We must make time in the exchange to let Him speak to us.

Consider the experience of Moses, that great man of God, in the land of Midian and, more specifically, at Horeb. He had doubtlessly passed that way several times before. However, on this occasion, he was confronted with a bush that was on fire though it was not consumed (Exod. 3:2). It was not until Moses turned aside to investigate that he realized that the fire was not about the bush. It was about God, seeking to get his attention. Meaningful communication can sometimes be hijacked by attention-getters. We become immersed in the means rather than in the end. We make the means into an end. For example, have you ever said the words, "I believe in prayer"? As if prayer is the beginning and end of it all. Prayer is simply a means through which we communicate with God, and it is in God that we believe, not so much in the means of prayer. Yes, prayer plays an important role, but, if we were *praying* to an idol, the result would not be the same. When Elijah and the prophets of Baal had a showdown on Mount Carmel, it was not the *means of communication* that made the difference. It was the *person* with whom they communicated.

Now let's get back to Moses. When Moses turned aside to investigate, he positioned himself in a place where he could hear God. It was only then that God spoke. Here is the exchange.

> So when the LORD saw that he turned aside to look, God called to him from the midst of the bush and said, "Moses, Moses!"

And he said, "Here I am."

Then He said, "Do not draw near this place. Take your sandals off your feet, for the place where you stand is holy ground." Moreover He said, "I am the God of your father—the God of Abraham, the God of Isaac; and the God of Jacob." And Moses hid his face for he was afraid to look upon God.

And the LORD said, "I have surely seen the oppression of My people who are in Egypt, and have heard their cry because of their taskmasters, for I know their sorrows. So I have come down to deliver them out of the hands of the Egyptians, and to bring them up from that land to a good and large land, to a land flowing with milk and honey, to the place of the Canaanites and the Hittites and the Amorites and the Perizites and the Hivites and the Jebusites. Now therefore, behold, the cry of the children of Israel has come to Me, and I have also seen the oppression with which the Egyptians oppress them. Come now, therefore, and I will send you to Pharaoh that you may bring My people, the children of Israel, out of Egypt." (Exod. 3:4–10)

Moses hid his face, for he was afraid to look upon God. This might seem rather strange. Yet, could it be that, by closing his eyes, Moses was simply shutting out the distraction of the fire so he could really listen to God? Haven't you been in conversation and ended up in a place where you have to ask yourself the question, *How did I ever get here?* I have done it several times. We allow ourselves to chase the proverbial rabbit and lose our way. Moses got the message that God was communicating to him, and he was terrified. Yes, terrified! Isn't that the reason we are sometimes afraid to listen to God—because we are afraid of what God might say or afraid of where God might send us or of what He might want us to do?

One of the most important aspects of communication is feeling that we have been heard. God knew that Moses heard him, but it was as if God were taken aback by the series of excuses Moses was making. Five times Moses tried to get out of the assignment, and five times God responded to him. The principle is clear: Don't give up too quickly. Moses was versed on using "I" statements. He refused to blame God for knocking at the wrong door but simply stated what he thought were legitimate reasons for his not wanting to go. *I'm not good enough. I don't know enough. I'm not credible enough. I'm not eloquent enough*, and, finally, *I really don't want to do this—send somebody else.*

Sometimes in communication, as in prayer, we send mixed messages. When what we say and what we do don't match, we must stop and ask ourselves the question, "What's going on?" We cannot say that we love the Lord and at the same time refuse to do what He says. He says, "If you love Me, keep My commandments" (John 14:15). We cannot say that we know that God is all-wise and then, when He tells us to do something, raise objections that would suggest that there are a number of things that God didn't think about when He gave the directive. God is speaking. Are you listening?

If we come to God only with what we want and are not open to what God might be saying to us, then we are not praying as we ought. When we read Scripture, what is our attitude? Do we read Scripture without seeking to bring our lives into alignment with it? When we cannot wait to raise our objections, we are not communicating with God but simply carrying on a parallel monologue. Since God speaks through Scripture, human relationships, nature, the Holy Spirit, and circumstances, we should always be sensitive to that reality. God could have spoken to Moses that day through one of the sheep, but instead He spoke from the burning bush. So, whenever and wherever we are, we should be open to hearing from God. God spoke to Adam and Eve in the Garden in the cool of the day (Gen. 3:8). He spoke to Abraham on several occasions and talked face to face with Moses. He gave military advice to Joshua and Jehoshaphat. To Solomon, Daniel, and a host of others, He spoke

> *If we come to God only with what we want and are not open to what God might be saying to us, then we are not praying as we ought*

in visions and dreams. If we are not careful, we can miss God's attempts to communicate with us.

We can be completely open with God because He understands. While from the human side of the exchange we need empathy, God does not need empathy from us. We can be completely open with Him because He knows everything about us, and He invites us to come to Him, not in shame but in confidence, as Paul points out: "For we do not have a High Priest who cannot sympathize with our weaknesses, but was in all points tempted as we are, yet without sin. Let us therefore come boldly to the throne of grace, that we may obtain mercy and find grace to help in time of need" (Heb. 4:15, 16).

Listening to God can be impeded by several things. These include: impatience, defensiveness, argument, an adversarial attitude, thinking that God doesn't love and doesn't want us to have any happiness or fun, aggression, believing that nothing good is ever going to happen, or simply playing games. We limit God when we act in a manner that is inconsistent with His will or in ways that suggest that, if it doesn't line up with human logic, it is not worth our time. Paul tells us that "whatever is not from faith is sin" (Rom. 14:23).

So, in an effort to be the best listener you can be, learn to control your thoughts, senses, and emotions. Speak directly and listen actively. God is always available. Jesus promised, "I will never leave you nor forsake you" (Heb. 13:5). "I will pray the Father, and He will give you another Helper, that He may abide with you forever, the Spirit of truth, whom the world cannot receive ... But the Helper, the Holy Spirit, whom the Father will send in My name, He will teach you all things, and bring to your remembrance all things that I said to you" (John 14:16, 17, 26).

Listening to the Holy Spirit is central to our faith and, as such, to our eternal destiny. Listening to the Spirit then is one way of expressing our love for Jesus. The Holy Spirit is the personal representative of Jesus who is charged with the responsibility of comforting, teaching, drawing, reminding, guiding, and assuring us. With this central role of the Holy Spirit, we cannot afford *not* to listen to Him. We must, therefore, take seriously the task of removing anything and everything that would inhibit our listening and learn to cultivate traits that would enhance our ability to listen.

When I began this chapter, I referred to the words of God Himself, "Be still, and know that I am God" (Ps. 46:10). In a world such as ours, with so many voices screaming at us, we have to make a conscious effort to tune into the voice of the Holy Spirit. We must be intentional in creating time and space for what some might refer to as "solitude." Jesus is our best example of the use of solitude. He would withdraw from human contact so that He could spend time alone with His Father. From such time with the Father He gained strength and power. Jesus would spend extended periods of time with His Father prior to making major decisions. I have found it to be of inestimable value to spend undisturbed time with God. In this regard, Ellen White made a statement that has had a profound impact on me, "When every other voice is hushed, and in quietness we wait before Him, the silence of the soul makes more distinct the voice of God" (*Christian Service*, p. 249). So, in my stillness, I'm intentional about inviting God to speak to me through His Holy Spirit. There have been times when God has been silent, and, of course, such silence is unsettling. As a result, I intentionally resist the urge to ignore God's silence. It could be that God is silent because He is waiting for me to follow through on a prior directive that I have not followed through on.

Obedience is one prerequisite for further revelation. God will not reward disobedience. I have learned not to ignore God's voice through the ministry of the Holy Spirit because it is by His ministry that I am sealed unto the day of redemption. Because listening to God has eternal consequences, I have no hesitation to say, "Speak Lord, for Your servant hears" (1 Sam. 3:9). I know that, when I listen to Him, I will never go wrong.

## Chapter 12

# PRAYER AND GOD'S WILL

If the answer to my prayer depends on it being in harmony with God's will and God knows what I need, why do I need to pray? Why doesn't God just go ahead and give me whatever it is that He thinks I should have. What if I don't know God's will for a particular area of my life? Would I just be wasting my time going through the motions?

In thinking about prayer, it seems to me that the will of God is very important if we are going to have the desired result. At least Jesus thinks so. As a precursor to what we often refer to as the Lord's Prayer, Jesus gives us a few prerequisites: Don't be like the hypocrites who love to pray in public. Pray in private. Don't use vain repetition. Be mindful that God knows what we need. Jesus then goes into the formal prayer.

> "Our Father in heaven, hallowed be Your name. Your kingdom come. Your will be done on earth as it is in heaven." (Matt. 6:9, 10)

It is not "our will be done in heaven" but God's "will be done on earth as it is done in heaven." So then, before we begin to ask for things, we should seek for a divine revelation of His will so that our request can be in compliance with God's purpose and not simply to fulfill our carnal desires.

But you might say, "Well, didn't Jesus say that we can ask whatever we will and His Father will give it to us? In fact, are there not many references that could give us that idea?" Let's look at a few of the verses that might seem to convey that idea.

"Ask, and it will be given to you; seek, and you will find; knock, and it will be opened to you. For everyone who asks receives, and he who seeks finds, and to him who knocks it will be opened." (Matt. 7:7, 8)

"Until now you have asked nothing in My name. Ask, and you will receive, that your joy may be full." (John 16:24)

"If you ask anything in My name, I will do it." (John 14:14)

"You did not choose Me, but I chose you and appointed you that you should go and bear fruit, and that your fruit should remain, that whatever you ask the Father in My name He may give you." (John 15:16)

While these verses might seem to infer that God is obligated to grant whatever we ask, that is not the case. John in his epistle says: "Now this is the confidence that we have in Him, that if we ask anything *according to His will*, He hears us" (1 John 5:14, emphasis added).

God's will is supreme. Therefore, God will not violate His will. Yet, we should be mindful that He wants the best for us. So, here is what He does—He provides help. "Likewise the Spirit also helps in our weaknesses. For we do not know what we should pray for as we ought, but the Spirit Himself makes intercession for us with groanings which cannot be uttered" (Rom. 8:26). "… Since He always lives to make intercession for them" (Heb. 7:25).

Jesus and the Holy Spirit both live to make intercession for us. Jesus is the Lamb slain from the foundation of the world, and He is from everlasting to everlasting. The Holy Spirit is also a member of the Godhead, which means that He was present before the foundation of the world. So, go ahead and pray your prayer, remembering that your words are not an end in themselves. God loves you too much to let you languish and die without meeting your needs. Jesus and the Holy Spirit make themselves responsible for ensuring that your prayer is presented to the Father in a manner that is acceptable.

Prayer always requires faith—faith in a God who hears, has the power, and is so in love with you that He would not say "yes" to a request that is outside of His will for you. When we pray within the will of God, we are honoring Him and giving Him the final word.

What do you do when your will is not in harmony with God's will? Do you stop praying? If you are like me, you might be inclined to do without or try to find some other source to have your need satisfied. However, I have just a word of encouragement—yes, a word of encouragement. You are in good company when you ask for something that you think might not be within the will of God. Even Jesus the Son of God asked for something that He felt might not be within the Father's will. (Remember Gethsemane?) So what did the Father do in that case?

> **Prayer always requires faith—faith in a God who hears, has the power, and is so in love with you that He would not say "yes" to a request that is outside of His will for you**

Before rushing to the answer, permit me to remind you that there was so much riding on the answer to Jesus' request that getting a "yes" would have placed years of experience in a complete state of flux. The redemption of the world was resting on the answer, while on the other hand, Jesus was facing death by crucifixion—a most horrible death. Paul wrote that God "made Him who knew no sin to be sin for us" (2 Cor. 5:21).

Let us return to the question, "What do you do when your will is not in harmony with the will of God?" and see how Jesus handled it. He removed Himself from all human association and distraction by going to His favorite place of prayer—the Mount of Olives. After His disciples had accompanied Him part way, He left them at a distance and fell on the ground in the stillness of the night, praying what may have been the most important prayer of His life on earth.

His prayer is recorded in Matthew 26:36–44.

## Prayer and God's Will

> Then Jesus came with them to a place called Gethsemane, and said to the disciples, "Sit here while I go and pray over there." And He took with Him Peter and the two sons of Zebedee, and He began to be sorrowful and deeply distressed. Then He said to them, "My soul is exceedingly sorrowful, even to death. Stay here and watch with Me." He went a little farther and fell on His face, and prayed, saying, "O My Father, if it is possible, let this cup pass from Me; nevertheless, not as I will, but as You will." Then He came to the disciples and found them sleeping, and said to Peter, "What! Could you not watch with Me one hour? Watch and pray, lest you enter into temptation. The spirit indeed is willing, but the flesh is weak." Again, a second time, He went away and prayed, saying, "O My Father, if this cup cannot pass away from Me unless I drink it, Your will be done." And He came and found them asleep again, for their eyes were heavy. So He left them, went away again, and prayed the third time, saying the same words.

When we ask over and over again for something that we think we really want, we are simply acting in harmony with our nature. Jesus asked several times, and the second and third times were even more intense. Luke provides us with added detail. He says that Jesus was in agony, and He prayed more earnestly. I'm not sure that we can truly understand the depth of Jesus' agony. "His sweat became like great drops of blood falling down to the ground" (Luke 22:44).

Jesus did not give up easily. Jesus was practicing what He taught His disciples to do—to be persistent in prayer. "Ask and keep on asking; seek and keep on seeking; and knock and keep on knocking. For everyone who asks will receive and whoever seeks will find and he who knocks the door will be opened" (Matt. 7:7, 8, paraphrase). When we don't seem to get the answer we desire, we tend to doubt the quality of our relationship with the Father. We conclude that there must be some sin in our lives. Maybe it is that we are not trusting Him enough. Maybe our faith is not strong enough, or maybe there is some other reason. However, when Jesus prayed in Gethsemane, He was still God, and His relationship with the Father was still completely intact. Yes, He was reluctant to take "no" for an answer. We, too, can have an intact relationship and be reluctant to take "no" for an answer—even when we have the nagging feeling that our request might not be the Father's will.

Knowing something intellectually and accepting it emotionally are quite different. Nothing is purely just one or the other, intellectual or emotional. However, here is what we can all learn from Jesus' experience. When our will clashes with God's will, we must do as He did; we must submit our will to His will. Remember, what we want, though different from what God wants, is not necessarily wrong. Refuse to live with guilt because your request was inappropriate and God said "no." Be willing to put it to rest by submitting to God's will. Why? Because God knows best and always has our best interest at heart. Jesus chose to go along with the Father's will and accept death by crucifixion. The pivotal word in His prayer was "nevertheless." Father, I don't feel like it, but *nevertheless* ... I don't want to, but *nevertheless* ..... When we trust the Father's love enough to say "nevertheless," we are well on our way to acknowledging God's rightful place in our lives.

If you are like me, even after I have resolved to surrender my will to God's will, I still feel upset. Four years after accepting my new assignment to pastor in a new city, I was still upset with God because He did not answer my prayer just the way I thought He should. I prayed, "Lord I have shoveled enough snow. I'm tired of shoveling snow. Please give me a church in an area where there is no snow and the church has no debt." In a matter of days after praying that prayer, I got a call from a friend of mine saying there were two churches open in Atlanta, and, he was wondering if I would like my name to be submitted. Of course, I said "yes." My name was submitted, and the rest is history. I interviewed for the position, the offer was made, and I accepted it.

Shortly after my arrival, I discovered that things were not all that I thought they would be. I did not get all the facts during the interview, and I was upset with God. However, it taught me a valuable lesson: When I pray, I should do so with the end in view. Whose end—mine or God's? God's end.

Into my fifth year, I began to see a new spirit and a new feeling in the church. It was a spirit of optimism and a feeling of hope.

Members were coming to me and saying, "Pastor, there is just something different about this year. This is going to be the year." God was ready to do a new thing, and I would be privileged to be a part of it.

I was attending one of our men's prayer breakfasts, and the first elder made the following comment: "I'm grateful for my pastor. I prayed for a pastor, and God gave me just the right person." He may not have noticed it, but tears welled up in my eyes, and I told God right then and there, "Thank You, God, for being patient with me. I may have wanted a church without debt, but You needed a pastor for this church and, in Your wisdom, I was that person." The debt is still there, but we are making strides in the right direction. God is being glorified, and the faith of many is being strengthened. "For I know the thoughts that I think toward you, says the LORD, thoughts of peace and not of evil, to give you a future and a hope" (Jer. 29:11).

Yes, God is thinking about me, and I have the confidence that, if I ask anything of Him, He hears me. However, it can at times be downright scary. What do the future and the hope He promises look like? For starters, I was driven back to the Word to discover what it had to say about God's will, and not just in relation to my job assignment, but also to all of life.

> "For this is the will of God, your sanctification: that you should abstain from sexual immorality; that each of you should know how to possess his own vessel in sanctification and honor, not in passion of lust, like the Gentiles who do not know God; that no one should take advantage of and defraud his brother in this matter, because the Lord is the avenger of all such, as we also forewarned you and testified. For God did not call us to uncleanness, but in holiness. Therefore he who rejects this does not reject man, but God, who has also given us His Holy Spirit." (1 Thess. 4:3–8)
>
> "In everything give thanks; for this is the will of God in Christ Jesus for you." (1 Thess. 5:18)
>
> "For this is the will of God, that by doing good you may put to silence the ignorance of foolish men." (1 Peter 2:15)

"See then that you walk circumspectly, not as fools but as wise, redeeming the time, because the days are evil. Therefore do not be unwise, but understand what the will of the Lord is. And do not be drunk with wine, in which is dissipation; but be filled with the Spirit, speaking to one another in psalms and hymns and spiritual songs, singing and making melody in your heart to the Lord, giving thanks always for all things to God the Father in the name of our Lord Jesus Christ, submitting to one another in the fear of God." (Eph. 5:17–21)

"And do not be conformed to this world, but be transformed by the renewing of your mind, that you may prove what is that good and acceptable and perfect will of God." (Rom. 12:2)

God's will is perfect, and we are to prove it in every area of our lives. How can we do this? By taking the time to discover God's will before we act in any area of life. Refrain from asking God for fresh revelations in any area concerning which He has already spoken. Take the time to do the research and come to the Scriptures with the heart of a learner. Here is a promise, God will always stand by: "If any of you lacks wisdom, let him ask of God, who gives to all liberally and without reproach, and it will be given to him. But let him ask in faith, with no doubting, for he who doubts is like a wave of the sea driven and tossed by the wind" (James 1:5, 6).

We can be sure that God wants to give good gifts to us—gifts that are for our long-term good. God gives us freedom of choice. He wants us to come to Him in faith, believing. This principle is illustrated in the experience of Solomon. I am encouraged by the way that Solomon responded to God's invitation and, in turn, how God granted Solomon's request.

## God's invitation to Solomon

God said to Solomon: "Ask! What shall I give you?"
Solomon responded: "You have shown great mercy to your servant David my father, because he walked before You in truth, in righteousness, and in uprightness of heart with You; You have continued this great kindness for him, and You have given him a son to sit on his throne, as it is this day. Now, O LORD my God, You have made Your servant king instead of

my father David, but I am a little child; I do not know how to go out or come in. And Your servant is in the midst of Your people whom You have chosen, a great people, too numerous to be numbered or counted. Therefore give to Your servant an understanding heart to judge Your people, that I may discern between good and evil. For who is able to judge this great people of Yours?" (1 Kings 3:6–9).

The speech pleased the Lord, that Solomon had asked this thing. Then God said to him: "Because you have asked this thing, and have not asked long life for yourself, nor have asked riches for yourself, nor have asked the life of your enemies, but have asked for yourself understanding to discern justice, behold, I have done according to your words; see, I have given you a wise and understanding heart, so that there has not been anyone like you before you, nor shall any like you arise after you. And I have also given you what you have not asked: both riches and honor, so that there shall not be anyone like you among the kings all your days. So if you walk in My ways, to keep My statutes and My commandments, as your father David walked, then I will lengthen your days." (1 Kings 3:10–14).

God might not always say "yes," but, whenever we align our request with His will, He will give us much more than we can ever ask or think. Praying God's will is one sure way to receive super abundant blessings.

## Chapter 13

# WHAT IF GOD ANSWERED ALL YOUR PRAYERS?

So many times I've had people ask me, "Pastor, why doesn't God answer my prayers?" "Pastor, would you pray for me? Maybe my faith is not strong enough." To the first question, I can usually provide a quick answer. Maybe it is because God knows better than you do or because He loves you too much to do for you what you are asking at this time. On the second question, I can do the first part in praying for the person but not without making a judgment on the person's faith, which I don't enjoy doing. God has given each person a measure of faith, and that faith grows as we walk in obedience to God's commands.

> *There is more to answered prayer than simply asking, seeking, and knocking. If that were all, then God would be nothing more than a robot or a vending machine*

The questioner sometimes comes back to me with the text from Matthew 7, "Ask and you will receive, seek and you will find, knock and it will be opened unto you." All that is true, but there is more to answered prayer than simply asking, seeking, and knocking. If that were all, then God would be nothing more than a robot or a vending machine. What would happen when there are conflicting requests? God is guided by His perfect will and not by our limited view of things. Another thing to remember is the love and wisdom of God. We should never forget that God loves us with an everlasting love, that He is drawing us with lovingkindness, and that His wisdom is beyond human comprehension. He is the Alpha and Omega, the Beginning and the End. His commitment to us is unquestionable. "Never will I leave you, never will I forsake you" (Heb. 13:5, BSB).

What if God answered prayers by human standards? For example, what if He answered according to whoever prays the longest or the hardest or according to whoever has been a Christian the longest, has the most faith, promises more, or sins less? When we pray, we must be mindful that God is guided by eternal unchanging principles. He is the same yesterday, today, and forever. He never contradicts Himself. All His divine attributes—holiness, righteousness, wisdom, knowledge, justice, love, power, presence, grace, mercy, and kindness—function in perfect harmony for His glory and for our good.

To ask God for something that we genuinely believe that we need and that He can give and then to not receive it can be downright frustrating and may even place our faith in a state of flux. However, let us be mindful that we do not know all that God knows. We ask according to our limited information and perspective, but God responds from His eternal perspective. "For I know the thoughts that I think toward you, says the LORD, thoughts of peace and not of evil, to give you a future and a hope" (Jer. 29:11). This one thing we can be sure of, God always has our best interest at heart. There are times when God will outrightly deny our request. Then there are other times when God will say, "Not yet," or He will deny the request because we are not quite ready to have it. God takes all the possible facts into consideration and always makes a wise, fair, just, loving, and consistent decision. God never makes a mistake.

Let's see if we can come to terms with God's response to our prayer, especially when He says "no," "wait," or "you are not ready." Even prophets in the Old Testament have had to deal with these three responses.

Take Balaam, for example, who was invited by King Balak to curse the children of Israel. When Balaam asked God about the invitation, God told him "no" because Israel was blessed. Balaam, short of throwing a temper tantrum, went back to God, and God gave him permission to go on the mission, with certain restrictions, of course. The outcome was that he almost lost his life, and, after four attempts to curse God's people, he was greatly embarrassed before the Moabites (Num. 22–24). A New Testament example is when Peter made an inappropriate request that was completely against the will of God, and God said, "No." Peter, James and John were on the Mount of Transfiguration, when Moses and Elijah appeared to Jesus. Seeing the heavenly visitors and the glory surrounding them, Peter wanted to stay there, so he sought permission to build booths. Jesus forbade him to do so (Matt. 17:1–8).

Another such example is one that seemed quite reasonable. James and John, along with their mother, came to Jesus requesting positions on the right and left side of Jesus in what they considered the soon-to-be-established kingdom. From their perspective, it was the thing to do. However, the request was based on wrong intelligence and selfish motives, so Jesus said "no" (Matt. 20:20–23).

Do you find yourself making the wrong request at times? Maybe even now you are struggling with the reality of a request that was denied several times. You might find the counsel given to Paul helpful. "My strength," God says to Paul, "is made perfect in weakness" (2 Cor. 12:9). Weakness! Who wants to be weak in a world that is so demanding? Who wants to be weak in a world where strength is so highly rated? Well, just think about the One whose strength is being perfected in your weakness. He is almighty, all-powerful, and full of compassion. His faithfulness is renewed every morning (Lam. 3:23).

What seems to be clear in these requests is that they were requests that were at cross-purposes with God's perfect will. God had already blessed Israel. Jesus did not intend to set up a kingdom on earth to subdue the Romans at that point in time, and, certainly, He had other plans for Paul. If these men, who were undeniably servants of God, were capable of making requests that were totally selfish, so are we. And God is too wise and too loving to grant purely self-serving requests. Really—think about it. Would you want a God who grants such shortsighted, materialistic, or inappropriate requests? We can all thank God for saying "no" to prayers that we all thought were perfectly reasonable when we prayed for them. However, as we look back, we now see what a disaster it would have been if He had said "yes."

We are usually slow—and even wrong—in assessing our own motives. We like to think that our motives are pure. But we often have wrong motives without even realizing it. Think about the relationships you have been in. Think about the problems you have had and when you have gone to God in prayer about them. Haven't you generally asked God to change the other person? We do it more frequently than we would probably care to admit. Jesus reminds us to take the beam out of our own eyes first so that we can see clearly to remove the speck out of the other person's eye (Luke 6:42).

How about admitting our unwillingness to face our own problems and shortcomings and letting God know that we would rather have the other person accommodate all our personal needs? When we refuse to face our shortcomings and want God to change others so that we can remain unchanged, God will certainly say "no."

So far we have seen that God has many reasons to say "no." God says "no" because He loves us too much to say "yes." He says "no" because He knows when our motives are not right. He says "no" because He knows that we are seeking our own glory and not His. Jesus reminds us that the kingdom, the power, and the glory belong to God forever. "I am the LORD, that is My name; and My glory I will not give to another, nor My praise to carved images" (Isa. 42:8).

When we ask God for things just so we can be compared more favorably with others, that is an inappropriate request. The student who wants to be on the dean's list simply to boast and not because he or she wishes to live up to his or her full potential is asking selfishly. God's purpose should be at the heart of every request that we make—God's glory, God's kingdom, God's mission in the world. When we look at our prayer requests through the lens of God's glory, kingdom, and mission in the world, it will purify our motives. When was the last time we confessed our wrong motives to God and asked for His forgiveness?

Persistence, though encouraged in Scripture, should not be viewed in isolation. There are times when persistence is persistence simply because we think our request is deserving of an answer in the affirmative and God has not been as responsive as we think He should be. However, God might be trying to get us to reexamine our motives or to revisit some unresolved issue in our lives. Sometimes persistence is our way of not dealing with character defects that need to be dealt with. Yet, here is something that might just fit your situation. God could have something better in mind. You could be only asking for *a place* in the kingdom when He really wants to give you the kingdom. Jesus said, "Do not fear little flock for it is your Father's good pleasure to give you the kingdom" (Luke 12:32).

Even though God is sovereign, Satan still has power to do harm to Christians. However, God will one day have the final say, and God is still able to take what Satan intended for our harm and make it out to be for our good. "And we know that all things work together for good to those who love God, to those who are the called according to His purpose" (Rom. 8:28). And, ultimately, at the second coming of Jesus, He "will wipe away every tear from their eyes; there shall be no more death, nor sorrow, nor crying. There shall be no more pain, for the former things have passed away" (Rev. 21:4).

How about God saying "not yet" so that we can develop a greater level of maturity? Oh how we hate to wait! We live in an instant society. Everything must be ready on demand. Needless to say, God can handle our impatience. God is not rattled by our insistence on things we want now. To insist on having things now is to suggest that we know better than God. If we know better than God, why do we go to Him for anything? As parents, there are certain good things that we would not give our children because, even though obedient, they might not have the level of maturity to appreciate the gift or to use it appropriately. A car is a good thing, but it is certainly inappropriate for a ten-year-old. Whenever God says, "wait," He has good reasons.

What might some of God's reasons be? For starters, how about His growing our faith in Him or simply testing the depth of our faith? Remember what the father who came to Jesus on behalf of his son said: "Lord, I believe; help my unbelief" (Mark 9:24). Or how about the mother who came to Jesus on behalf of her daughter? When Jesus said, "It is not right to take the children's bread and toss it to dogs" (Matt. 15:26, NIV), she responded in faith: "Yes, Lord, yet even the little dogs eat the crumbs which fall from their master's table" (Matt. 15:26, 27).

God might have us wait so that we can reexamine our request and make the necessary changes. While the Bible does not mention it explicitly, I cannot help but think that Joseph must have asked over and over again to be given the opportunity to go back home to see his father. However, years later, we see him saying to his brothers, "You meant evil against me; but God meant it for good, in order to bring it about as it is this day, to save many people alive" (Gen. 50:20). Let's look at Jesus' prayer in the garden: "If it be possible let this cup pass from me, nevertheless not my will but Thine be done" (Luke 22:42, paraphrase). It seems as though there were no lapse in time, yet His desire to have the will of His Father be dominant was far more important than His own. When we live our lives with a view to allowing God's will to be supreme in our lives, waiting will not be a problem for us. We will count it all joy.

When God says, "wait," He might just be placing us in a spot where we can develop character traits that are in line with His character. We develop character when we deal with pain, hurt, struggle, disappointment, rejection, and other setbacks. We certainly would not mind going through life without these struggles, but, in the wisdom of God, there is more than adequate reason for them. I am always mindful of God's statement in Isaiah 55:8, 9: "For My thoughts are not your thoughts, nor are your ways My ways," says the LORD. "For as the heavens are higher than the earth, so are My ways higher than your ways, and My thoughts than your thoughts." The thoughts that God has towards us are "thoughts of peace and not of evil, to give us a future and a hope" (Jer. 29:11).

Simply put, God says, "Wait," because He is sovereign. God's ultimate purpose is that we grow into His likeness. The real purpose of salvation is to restore in us the image of our Maker. Let's think about the difference that it would make in all of our relationships if we were truly like our Maker. The fact of the matter is that we are *not* like Him and, consequently, we are sometimes our own worst enemy. We block the answer to our prayers.

Let's visit our prayer life. Do we have a series of unanswered prayers? Does the sovereign God have to keep on saying to us "no," or "not yet"? The way to have a paradigm shift is to walk in obedience to God. When we walk in obedience to God, we position ourselves where God can give us additional blessings.

When you pray, be mindful of God's ability. Nothing is impossible with God. Yet, God is not just interested in giving us things; He is interested in our becoming like Him. He wants us to be in a right relationship with Him. God wants a change of mind in us. He wants us to be transformed by the renewing of our minds. Paul counsels: "Let this mind be in you which was also in Christ Jesus" (Phil. 2:5). Transformation comes our way by our granting the all-powerful God permission. This means a change of attitude toward strained relationships and a harsh spirit. It means acknowledging the need for repentance and giving and receiving forgiveness. When our relationships with God and our fellowmen are right, God will open the floodgates of heaven and pour us out blessings that there will not be room enough to receive them. We will be blessed in our going out and in our coming in. God's blessing will overtake us (Deut. 28:1–6). When the request is right, when the timing is right and you are right, God says, "Yes." Remove the obstacles, and the answers will keep coming. I am so glad that God does not say, "yes," to all my prayers. When God's answers defy my senses

> **When you pray, be mindful of God's ability. Nothing is impossible with God**

and experience, I must accept that He sees what I cannot, that He knows what I do not, that He chooses more wisely than I could ever choose, and that He answers my prayers in the best possible manner.

## TEACH Services, Inc.
### PUBLISHING

We invite you to view the complete
selection of titles we publish at:
**www.TEACHServices.com**

We encourage you to write us
with your thoughts about this,
or any other book we publish at:
**info@TEACHServices.com**

TEACH Services' titles may be purchased in
bulk quantities for educational, fund-raising,
business, or promotional use.
**bulksales@TEACHServices.com**

Finally, if you are interested in seeing
your own book in print, please contact us at:
**publishing@TEACHServices.com**

We are happy to review your manuscript at no charge.